S

Plea
show

Rer

Tex
spe

www

Paul Atterbury's
Lost
Railway
Journeys

The Steam Tram, Ehn R

Paul Atterbury's

Lost
Railway
Journeys

D&C
David and Charles

A DAVID & CHARLES BOOK

© F&W Media International LTD 2011
David & Charles is an imprint of F&W Media International, LTD
Brunel House, Forde Close, Newton Abbot, TQ12 4PU, UK

F&W Media International, LTD is a subsidiary of F+W Media, Inc., 4700 East
Galbraith Road
Cincinnati OH45236, USA

First published in the UK in 2011
Copyright © Paul Atterbury 2011

Paul Atterbury has asserted his right to be identified as author of this work in
accordance with the Copyright, Designs and Patents Act, 1988.

Entries in this publication were originally published in the following titles:
Branchline Britain, *Along Lost Lines* and *Along Country Lines*.

ISBN-13: 978-1446300954
ISBN-10: 1-4463-0095-1

Printed in China RR Donnelley for:
F&W Media International, LTD
Brunel House, Forde Close, Newton Abbot, TQ12 4PU, UK

Commissioning Editor Neil Baber
Senior Editor Verity Muir
Senior Designer Mia Trenoweth
Design Sue Cleave
Production Manager Beverley Richardson

F+W Media publishes high quality books on a wide range of subjects.
For more great book titles visit: **www.rubooks.co.uk**

Contents

Introduction

During the 1960s and early 1970s the railway map of Britain was devastated by closures and many parts of the country were left without any kind of railway service. The main inspiration for this was the publication in 1963 of Dr Richard Beeching's famous report, entitled The Reshaping of British Railways. The direct result of this report was the closure of over 2000 stations and many thousands of miles of track, in effect halving the network that had been inherited from the Victorians. However, Dr Beeching was not the first to recommend the closing of railway lines and stations. The earliest closures took place in the 1840s and in the 1920s and 1930s over 3000 route miles were lost throughout Britain. Lines were also lost during the 1950s.

Most of these early closures, of largely minor, remote or duplicated lines, passed without comment and it was not until the Beeching axe began to fall that the public began to fight, generally in vain, to save lines and stations threatened with closure.

▶ A particularly attractive railway walk is along the Meon valley in Hampshire. Plenty of railway reminders remain, such as this bridge across the Meon at Soberton.

The railway timetables of the 1950s and early 1960s are filled, therefore, with journeys now either impracticable or impossible, and the landscape of Britain is littered with the remains of abandoned railways. In some cases the route survives, complete with viaducts and bridges, cuttings and embankments, tunnels and fragments of stations and other buildings. All that is missing is the track and the trains. In others, all has been swept away, leaving little to suggest that the railway ever existed. However, the routes are often marked on Ordnance Survey maps and so these are the key to any exploration of the lost railways of Britain. Walking old railways is now a national past time, thanks to books, television programmes and rambling clubs and, through the efforts of organisations such as Sustrans, many lost railways are now enjoying a new life as official footpaths and cycle ways. Many miles of lost lines have also been saved as preserved or heritage railways and, in a few cases, closed lines have been reopened as part of the national network.

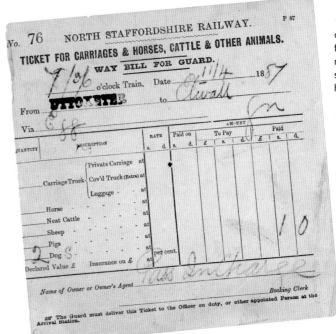

◄ The movement of animals from farm to market, and for slaughter, was a huge business: in 1913, the total was nearly 20 million animals. Horses were also important, with special horseboxes for race horses, complete with groom's compartment.

▶ This colourful Edwardian card was issued by the Caledonian Railway to draw attention to its special trains carrying newsprint for the Glasgow Evening News. Railway publicity at the time made much of freight, and official cards such as these indicate the importance of freight services at a time when they were at their peak.

Introduction

This book is about closed lines and lost journeys. It is also about memory, nostalgia and imagination. Every part of Britain was affected by the Beeching era but country areas suffered the most, notably in East Anglia, the West Country, Wales and Scotland. Branch lines and rural routes were particularly hard hit and so these feature strongly in the book. The lines and journeys are arranged regionally, and have been selected to show the diversity and variety of the routes that were lost and the equally diverse and often unexpected things that remain. They are depicted in their heyday as operating railways and as surviving fragments so be discovered and enjoyed in the landscape, by the generations that knew them and by those for whom the age of steam is simply a romantic part of Britain's history.

The West Country
1 Lynton & Barnstaple Railway
2 Yelverton to Princetown
3 Axminster to Lyme Regis
4 Maiden Newton to Bridport
5 Taunton to Barnstaple
6 Evercreech Junction to
   Burnham-on-Sea

Southern England
7 Dunton Green to Westerham
8 Paddock Wood to Hawkhurst
9 Chippenham to Calne
10 The Isle of Wight
11 Longmoor Military Railway

East Anglia
12 Saxmundham to Aldeburgh
13 Kelvedon to Tollesbury
14 Spalding to Yarmouth
15 Peterborough to King's Lynn
16 Mid Suffolk Light Railway

Central England
17 Wantage Tramway
18 Stonehouse to Nailsworth
19 Woodhall Junction to Horncastle
20 Buxton to Ashbourne and High Peak
   Junction
21 Cheltenham to King's Sutton
22 Cheltenham to Andover

Wales
23 Whitland to Cardigan
24 Gaerwen to Amlwch
25 Ruabon to Barmouth and Blaenau
   Ffestiniog
26 Carmarthen to Aberystwyth

Northern England
27 Alne to Easingwold
28 Skipton to Grassington
29 Abbey Town to Silloth
30 Derwent Valley Light Railway
31 Cockermouth to Sellafield

Scotland
32 Castle Douglas to Kirkcudbright
33 Roxburgh to Jedburgh
34 Killin Junction to Loch Tay
35 Dunblane to Crianlarich
36 Aberdeen to Ballater

Lynton and Barnstaple Railway, Blackmoor Gate Station.

The West Country

SOUTH WESTERN AND MIDLAND RAILWAY COMPANIES'
SOMERSET AND DORSET JOINT LINE.
(CARRIAGE NOTE.) ALFRED PEACE, (512)
GOODS DEPARTMENT, Carriage Agent, Station, 16 / 4 / 190
M Slay NORWICH ROAD,
Dr. To the SOU... BOURNEMOUTH, WEST.

KING TOR
PLATFORM

Lynton & Barnstaple Railway

Few local railways attract as much interest as the Lynton & Barnstaple. In any case, narrow-gauge lines were something of a rarity in England, particularly ones whose primary inspiration was the carriage of passengers rather than freight.

Lynton and Barnstaple Railway, Blackmoor Gate Station.

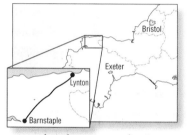

The railway's long and meandering 2ft-gauge line was opened in May 1898, and from the start it made a significant contribution to the tourist development of Lynton, Lynmouth and the remote coastline of north Devon. Smart, well run and with great local support, the Lynton & Barnstaple soon made its mark, despite the fact that its trains took up to an hour and a half to complete the 19-mile journey. Travellers benefited from the direct connection with the main line at Barnstaple Town station. In 1923 the line became part of the Southern Railway, and its locomotives were repainted in SR green. By this time, however, the railway was already suffering from road competition, and by the end of the decade freight traffic had almost gone and motor coaches were making serious inroads into the passenger carrying. By the early 1930s, closure was an ever-present threat, but when it came, with little warning, on 30 September 1935 there was local outrage.

However, an ambitious preservation society was formed in 1979 and

▲ This 1920s postcard shows Blackmoor Gate station, midway between Lynton and Barnstaple. The popularity of the line was reflected in the number of postcards produced in this period, showing the stations, the trains and the line in the north Devon landscape. The stations were built to a pattern, echoing the Arts and Crafts styling in fashion when the line was built. Today, Blackmoor Gate station is a pub.

▶ In September 1933 one of the line's distinctive Manning Wardle tank locomotives stands at the head of its train while the few passengers take their seats for the leisurely journey from Lynton to Barnstaple. A local resident, possibly the writer Henry Williamson, who was a great supporter of the line, chats with the driver.

[12]

▶ One day the Lynton & Barnstaple Railway may reopen the whole length of its original route, but at the moment much of the trackbed is hidden in the landscape, waiting to be discovered by intrepid explorers with good maps. Confrontations with local residents are not uncommon. Much of the route is, in any case, on private land.

has been working on plans to reopen the line. Being small and lightly engineered, much of the trackbed quickly disappeared back into the landscape. But bridges and other structures survive, notably the great Chelfham viaduct, as well as some stations converted to private houses. In 2004 the first steam trains operated from Woody Bay since 1935.

▲ The Lynton & Barnstaple is coming back to life. Woody Bay station has been fully restored and trains are running on a section of relaid track. In April 2004 the locomotive 'Emmet' poses at the platform at Woody Bay.

Yelverton to Princetown

Today the idea of a railway into the remote heart of Dartmoor seems both curious and unlikely, yet such an idea was planted and took root right at the start of railway history.

The first part of a horse-drawn railway from Plymouth to Princetown was authorized in 1819, and four years later 23 miles of track opened between Sutton Pool and King Tor. The name of the railway's promoter, politician and diplomat Sir Thomas Tyrwhitt, lives on in the Tyrwhitt Trail, the footpath and cycleway that follows the route. His plan was

▲ King Tor Platform was one of England's most inaccessible stations. A particular passion among some enthusiasts was visiting obscure stations. Here, in the 1950s, two well-dressed and well-heeled rail buffs cross King Tor off their list, without an anorak to be seen.

▼ Freight was important throughout the life of the Princetown branch, and mixed passenger and freight trains ran regularly. Here, in the 1950s, the freight wagons are shunted while the single coach waits in the platform. Today only the houses on the left remain.

G. W. R.

PRINCETOWN

to transport stone from local quarries down to Plymouth, bringing back manure and materials to develop the moor. It was largely defunct by the 1860s, but a 10-mile section between Yelverton, on the main Tavistock to Plymouth line, and Princetown was revived by the GWR as the Princetown Railway. This was opened on 11 August 1883. Although instigated and operated by the GWR, it remained nominally independent until 1922.

Closure came in the 1960s, along with most of the main line to Plymouth via Okehampton and Tavistock. However, much of the branch line's trackbed remained. Now, part of it makes a glorious walk across the moors. There is not much to see around Yelverton, but from Dousland the route is spectacular, passing Burrator Reservoir and then climbing into increasingly empty moorland to reach the desolation of King Tor before dropping down to Princetown.

▶ It is near the end of the line's life in the early 1960s, and the mixed train sets off from Burrator, leaving a single passenger on the wooden platform. Today the line has gone, but the views across the reservoir and around its wooded shores are as good as ever.

▼ Much of the trackbed remains today as an exciting footpath and cycleway winding its way across Dartmoor through a wonderfully remote landscape. The circuitous route, particularly the great loop around King Tor, is a legacy of the first railway, built in the early 1820s.

Axminster to Lyme Regis

When it opened in August 1903, the Lyme Regis branch line had already enjoyed a chequered history. Plans for a railway to Lyme were first drawn up in the 1840s, the first of many schemes to be developed during the Victorian era.

◄ A single-coach train has arrived hauled by the characteristic Adams 4-4-2 radial tank engines at Lyme Regis. Meanwhile the solitary passenger prepares to hand her ticket to the station master.

In September 1874 the first sod for the line was ceremoniously cut, but that was as far as it got. Eventually, the passing of the Light Railways Act in 1896, which encouraged the building of many rural railways, inspired the formation of the Axminster & Lyme Regis Railway, and in 1897 work started on the construction of the line. There were problems with engineering and

▼ The route from Axminster to Lyme included one intermediate stop at Combpyne, a station very much in the middle of nowhere. This 1950s colour photograph shows a typical single-coach train on its way to Lyme, hauled by an Adams radial tank locomotive, the mainstay of the line for thirty years. In the background is the camping coach that was stabled at Combpyne over many years, offering notably quiet holidays. The one local attraction was the landslip at Downland Cliffs.

London and South Western Ry. 787
FROM WATERLOO TO
COMBPYNE

◀ This Edwardian postcard shows quite a substantial train making its way through the woods near Combpyne. This part of the route was particularly attractive, with many lineside flowers. On the card these look like rhododendrons but, as it is hand-coloured, this may be artistic licence.

CELEBRITIES OF

Duke of Monmouth, 1685.   *Jane Austen, novelist.*

LYME REGIS.

◀ An unusual combination of celebrities come together on this card, made to promote Lyme Regis before World War I. The Duke of Monmouth is not everyone's hero, and Jane Austen was not as popular at that time as she is now. Mary Anning, an early student of prehistory and a great fossil hunter, was the true Lyme heroine.

finance, but the line finally opened to great local celebrations, despite the fact that the station was half a mile from the town and 250ft above sea level. The line was operated from the start by the London & South Western Railway Company, which took over complete control in 1907.

Successful and popular during the Edwardian era and between the wars, the railway saw a boom in both passenger traffic and freight, and helped to put Lyme on the map as a tourist resort. In 1914 a magazine described the resort as 'highly esteemed by visitors desiring holidays of a quieter kind, and those who reckon scenic, climatic and natural attractions as of greater value than bandstands and the

like…'. At its peak, the service included twelve trains a day each way, some of which were through trains to and from London.

Decline began in the 1950s, as a result of increasing competition from road transport. British Railways improved the track and introduced diesel railcars, but to no avail. By the early 1960s some trains were carrying an average of only two passengers. Closure, hastened by the Beeching Report, became inevitable. The last train ran on 29 November 1965.

▶ Many long-lost branch lines are now little more than a walk through the woods, the only clue to their previous life sometimes being old lineside concrete fencing posts hidden in the bushes. Often these lost lines look their best in winter and early spring, with the soft sunlight filtering through the trees, and the autumn leaves still under foot.

▲ The hilly route made demands on the line's builders but these were mostly overcome without massive expenditure. At Cannington, however, a ten-arch viaduct presented a major challenge. One of the first to be constructed from concrete, and the second highest of its kind in Britain, the viaduct caused engineering and financial problems that delayed the railway's opening. One arch subsided and had to be additionally supported. Today, long after the line's closure, the viaduct still strides across the valley, a permanent memorial to the trains that once ran to Lyme Regis.

The route from Axminster to Lyme Regis

Winding its way through the landscape on a steeply graded track, the Lyme Regis branch in its early days was hard on both locomotives and drivers, and the short journey rarely took less than 25 minutes. However, there were few complaints as the scenery along the route was exciting and varied, with plenty of good views across the Dorset hills and valleys. In any case, the railway opened up an area hitherto relatively inaccessible. In many ways a classic branch line, in its latter years the route attracted many passengers who simply wanted to experience the kind of journey that was soon to be extinct.

A couple of years after closure the track was lifted, and the railway began to disappear back into the landscape. Various schemes to reopen the

◀ Popular since the late eighteenth century, and made famous by Jane Austen, Lyme Regis was known as a relatively undeveloped and quiet resort, famous for its fossils, its fishing and its exceptional setting. The railway did little to change this, for the resort continued to offer the kind of holiday that had little appeal to mass tourism. This advertisement of the 1930s, while listing many conventionally desirable holiday features, still manages to suggest that Lyme was somehow different.

▼ It is a sunny day in the 1950s and a typical single-coach train has arrived at Lyme Regis, hauled by one of the line's characteristic Adams 4-4-2 radial tank engines. These venerable survivors of the Victorian era were designed by William Adams while he was the locomotive superintendent of the London & South Western Railway. Even in the 1950s they were popular with railway enthusiasts, as indicated by the boy in the foreground taking a photograph. Meanwhile the solitary passenger prepares to hand her ticket to the station master.

line have been announced, but to no avail, even though Lyme Regis is one of those small towns that would benefit enormously from a complete ban on cars in its crowded centre.

What remains today

Today it is quite hard to explore the remains of the line. Much is now private and inaccessible, and considerable sections have disappeared. The remains of the bay platform can still be seen at Axminster, a station whose recent restoration has given it a Victorian look. It also boasts one of the best station cafés in southern Britain. The location of Combpyne station can also be traced, as well as the route through the woods. Some of the bridges survive, spanning overgrown cuttings, but Lyme Regis station has vanished without trace. The best, and most accessible, feature is the great viaduct at Cannington.

Maiden Newton to Bridport

A number of branch lines in the south-west were built by small, independent companies set up by local merchants and businessmen keen to expand trade by linking their towns and villages to the national railway network.

◀ A four-coach train hurries along the line towards Bridport's East Street station.

Typical was the Bridport Railway, whose 9-mile line to Maiden Newton opened amid great local celebration on 11 November 1857. Initially a broad-gauge line to suit its GWR surroundings, it was later rebuilt to standard gauge. Independence was short lived, for within a year or so the line was leased to the Great Western. In 1901 the GWR took complete control, and continued to operate it until the British Railways era.

In 1884 the line was extended to Bridport harbour, a busy local trading and fishing port. This reflected the ambitions of the GWR, which was keen to develop a harbour and port that could rival Weymouth. Thinking also of the developing tourist trade, the company renamed the harbour West Bay and hoped that the hotels would soon arrive, inspired by the beautiful coast and the new railway link. In the event, not much happened, and West Bay remained much the same as before, a small but busy local port. However, the carriage of beach gravel became a mainstay of the line and remained so until the closure of the West Bay extension in 1962.

► The route of the West Bay extension along the valley of the Brit from Bridport town, visible in the distance, to the harbour, just off the picture to the left, can clearly be seen. Here, in the 1920s, a locomotive shunts on the siding while carriages and a gravel train wait in the platform.

▼ In the 1960s a single diesel railcar pauses at Toller. Two ladies, probably back from a shopping trip to Maiden Newton – and clearly not the focus of the photographer's interest – leave the train. Today, the platform survives, as does the road bridge just beyond the station, but all around are new houses.

GREAT WESTERN RAILWAY. (135 a)

TOLLER
TO
SHEFFIELD L.N.E.

| No. of Packages | CARRIAGE PAID |

Route via

G. W. R.

Bridport

▲ With closure in 1975 still relatively recent, much of the Bridport branch survives in the landscape. Parts of the route are walkable, others are private, but the route can easily be traced through the valleys and up over the Dorset hills. There are some unexpected survivals to be seen, such as this former platelayer's hut beside the trackbed.

Always popular with local users, the Bridport branch enjoyed a busy service. Indeed, in the early days of the West Bay extension a special bathing train left Bridport at seven each morning. In the early 1960s there were twenty trains each way on weekdays. Steam gave way to diesel and services carried on. The line survived the Beeching plan and by the early 1970s had escaped a number of closure schemes, its Houdini-like behaviour giving rise to plenty of local support and optimism. However, it was all in vain, and full closure came in May 1975 – one of Britain's last branch line closures. Had the line lived on for another couple of years, it would surely have survived.

What there is to see today

Today there are plenty of remains to be seen. West Bay station survives, but both Bridport's stations have gone. A solitary crossing gate just outside the town is the town's railway memorial. The steeply graded route followed valleys through the hills up to Maiden Newton and can easily be identified from nearby minor roads. Cuttings, embankments and bridges survive, along with platforms at Powerstock and Toller, the only intermediate stations. Powerstock station always looked like a private house, and that is now exactly what it is. At Maiden Newton station there are still trains, on the Weymouth to Bristol route. This was the service that used to connect with the Bridport branch, whose trains waited in the bay platform. For those wanting to travel from Bridport in any other direction, notably to London, the journey was tortuous and involved a number of changes. This makes it even more remarkable that this essentially local railway kept going for so long.

▶ In the late 1980s West Bay station was a sorry sight, derelict and tumbledown, and the platform was used as a store for old boats and marine bits and pieces. Since then this pretty stone building, built in the typical vernacular style of rural Dorset stations, has been fully restored and given a new lease of life as a café. Track has been relaid beside the platform, a signal has been erected, and the trackbed towards Bridport has been turned into a public footpath.

(*Inset*) In 1908 a four-coach train, hauled by the type of GWR tank locomotive long associated with the branch, hurries along the line towards Bridport's East Street station, having left West Bay a few minutes earlier. A road has buried this part of the route.

G.W.R. WEST BAY BRANCH.

Taunton
to Barnstaple

On 1 November 1873 the first train from Taunton steamed slowly into the newly completed wooden terminus buildings of Barnstaple Victoria Road, to the east of Barnstaple's town centre. The railway scheme, authorized in 1864, had taken nearly ten years to construct the 43 miles required.

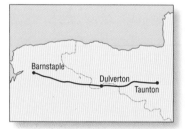

The builder was the Devon & Somerset Railway, an independent company backed by the Bristol & Exeter, who were keen to push their broad-gauge network westwards into north Devon. In effect a long branch line, it was cheaply built and initially had only three passing points. Services were, as a result, chaotic, but things improved in 1881 when it was all converted to standard gauge. Six years later a short spur was opened to link it to Barnstaple Junction, the terminus station of the LSWR's line from Exeter. The inspiration for this was the railway from Barnstaple to Ilfracombe, completed in 1874, which had brought rapid growth and much holiday traffic to that north Devon resort. This spur enabled trains from Taunton, and thus from many parts of central Britain, to run through to Ilfracombe. At this point the GWR, keen to expand its holiday and freight traffic at the

▲ Taunton can be identified from many directions by its great church tower, as this card makes clear. The station is away from the town centre but there are views over the town from west-bound trains going towards the junction by Norton Fitzwarren, where the lines to Minehead and to Barnstaple branched away. The Minehead line survives as a preserved railway.

▶ The Devon & Somerset was essentially a local line serving remote areas, and built rather slowly with a small budget. However, the landscape demanded some comparatively expensive engineering, including large river bridges. Today the iron girders are long gone but stone support pillars or approach arches survive. This, looking like some overgrown medieval ruin, is the approach arch to the former crossing of the Exe.

expense of its great rival, the LSWR, took an interest and in 1901 bought the Devon & Somerset company. Later improvements allowed GWR trains to bypass Victoria Road, with the result that traffic to the station diminished and it was eventually closed and demolished. By this time, centrally placed Barnstaple Town had been the main station for some years, so Victoria Road was in any case redundant.

Apart from the holiday trains, the only traffic of any significance was that servicing the needs of local agriculture, including the carriage of both cattle and rabbits. The single-track line took a rural route that managed to avoid most of the villages and small towns along the way. Dulverton and South Molton, the only places of substance, were both some distance from the railway, and most of the other intermediate stations served small and remote villages. The landscape is hilly, cut by deep river valleys, so some expensive engineering was required, including three tunnels and substantial iron girder bridges over the Mole, the Exe and the Tone. Construction may have been done cheaply, but care was taken with finish and detailing, notably frequent use of rough-cut local stone. It was a leisurely, delightful journey through a lovely landscape, with distant views of Exmoor. However, that was not enough

▼ Wiveliscombe station was the second stop on the line and the station was, for once, fairly near the little town it served. On a late summer's afternoon in 1963 the Barnstaple train pulls in. Although closure is threatening, the station is still looking tidy.

▲ Dulverton was a substantial station with extensive freight facilities including a large goods shed. However, as this 1963 photograph suggests, it was a long way from the town. Today, the main station building, the goods shed and some of the platforms survive, along with an old railway hotel that has been converted into apartments.

▲ The railway has left its mark on the glorious landscape. Here, its route can be identified in the middle distance as a straight line of trees along the valley of the Yeo, with the hills around Molland in the distance.

to generate significant income and it was really only the holiday traffic to Ilfracombe and other north Devon resorts that kept the line open. Closure was inevitable, and it finally came in October 1966.

The route today

Sections of the old railway line have been lost to farming, road building and into people's back gardens, and many bridges have gone, but some handsome stone stations and other buildings survive, notably at Dulverton. Considerably altered, by contrast, is the site of Morebath Junction, from where a short connecting branch ran south to Tiverton via Bampton, allowing access to north Devon from Exeter and the south. Sadly, much of the route is today relatively inaccessible and private, though it can easily be identified and followed from minor roads. Comparatively apparent are sections that have been taken over as farm access tracks. The landscape is constantly appealing and varied as the

▲ The end of the line, literally, at Barnstaple Victoria Road, the former terminus of the Devon & Somerset Railway: closure is imminent, and even the station name board is falling apart.

line winds its way through the hills; it would make a glorious long-distance footpath. Inevitably, the rural and remote nature of the line has meant that many sections are overgrown and impenetrable, but those that are accessible have a distinct sense of hidden mystery, heightened by the usual elements that identify any lost railway, such as concrete fence posts, old wooden gates and traces of platelayers' huts. However, deep in the peaceful Devon countryside, it is hard to visualize those holiday expresses charging by.

Evercreech Junction to Burnham-on-Sea

Somerset was well served by railways in the nineteenth century, particularly in the largely rural triangle formed by Bristol, Taunton and Yeovil. Some of these, like the canals that preceded them, were inspired by the Somerset coal fields but, that apart, there was little industry in the region.

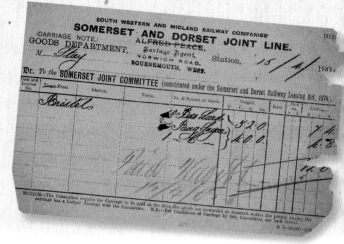

Coastal harbours and ports and river estuaries were still busy, and they fuelled the hopes of railway promoters. In the 1850s several railway companies were authorized, including the East Somerset, the West Somerset and the Somerset Central. Another scheme under way in this region was the Dorset Central, whose line from Wimborne to Cole was completed early in 1862. By this time, the Somerset Central had opened its line from Highbridge to Glastonbury, with

▲ Always independently minded, the S&D has long been the favourite of many enthusiasts. Surviving paperwork, such as this 1900s carriage note from Bournemouth goods department, is much sought after.

▼ Glastonbury and Street was a substantial station, for it was here that the Wells branch met the Highbridge line. On this occasion, probably in the 1920s, things were quiet and the photographer could take his time.

Today there is little to indicate that Evercreech was ever a busy railway junction, yet it was here that in 1874 the new Somerset & Dorset main line to Bath met the existing Highbridge line. Sheep now graze in the empty fields where mighty locomotives used to meet. Here, in October 1965, a Bournemouth-to-Bristol express pauses at Evercreech Junction beside the local for Highbridge.

branches to Burnham pier and Wells, plus a later extension eastwards towards Cole. This was originally a broad-gauge line, supported by the Bristol & Exeter, and thus the GWR. In the early 1860s it was converted to standard gauge and merged with the Dorset Central to form the famous Somerset & Dorset Railway in 1862. Ambitious plans to extend north to Bath from Evercreech were undermined by financial problems and, though completed in 1874, bankruptcy soon followed and the network was leased by the Midland and the London & South Western, who formed the Somerset & Dorset Joint Railway. While the Bath-to-Bournemouth route became the main line, Highbridge remained important, not least because the company's works was located there. A century after they were built, in the 1960s, most of Somerset's railways were swept away, including the Somerset & Dorset. The main line and the branch from Evercreech to Highbridge closed in 1966.

From Evercreech to Glastonbury there is not much to be seen today and the surviving trackbed and stations, at Pylle and West Pennard, are on private land. West of Glastonbury the route is a cycleway and footpath (Sustrans Route 3) as far as Shapwick. Old bridges include one over the River Brue. At Edington Route 3 turns away to follow the Bridgwater branch. Nothing remains at Highbridge or Burnham.

▶ Sometimes unexpected survivals, such as this level-crossing gatepost west of Glastonbury, are the only things to indicate that there was once a railway there.

▼ (Overleaf) When railways are closed, the track and much of the infrastructure, particularly the metalwork, soon disappear. This metal bridge west of Glastonbury survives, now used for farm access.

◄ Standing on the footbridge, this photographer appears to have taken great care with the arrangement of his picture of Highbridge level crossing, posing the signalman and the pedestrians and catching the horse and cart at the right moment. Signals show that no trains were due.

► Edington Burtle, seen here in October 1965, was a typical S&D country station, marking the junction with the line south to Bridgwater.

▼ Much of the route westwards from Evercreech can be identified, though access is not always possible. Here, near West Pennard, the line of the trackbed can still be seen, now used as a farm access track.

Southern England

COUNTRY AFTERNOON
TICKETS

FROM LONDON AND SUBURBS

062

0690

LONGMOOR MILITARY RAILWAY
OPEN DAY - 3rd JUNE, 1967
Valid for travel between LISS,
LONGMOOR DOWNS & OaKHANGER
and via HOLLYWATER LOOP
For conditions see over
Williamson, Ticket Printer, Ashton-u-Lyne

Dunton Green to Westerham

On 7 July 1881, amid great local celebrations, a 5-mile branch line was opened to link Westerham with the South Eastern Railway main line at Dunton Green. Conceived as a longer route along the valley below the North Downs to meet another main line at Oxted, the railway never progressed beyond Westerham.

Hill Climb, Westerham, Kent.

This small market town, the birthplace of General Wolfe, victor at Quebec, benefited greatly from the coming of the railway. Shops and businesses flourished and, more importantly, tourists arrived, often with their bicycles, to explore the Kent and Surrey borders and the Pilgrim's Way. As Westerham was only 26 miles from both Charing Cross and Cannon Street, the railway had the advantage of being one of the few rural branch lines easily and quickly accessible from central London, something that continued to attract passengers, and later railway enthusiasts, throughout the lifetime of the line. A journey time to London of under an hour also meant that the branch was used by commuters. In the 1920s there were at least fifteen trains in each direction on weekdays. Passengers on the first train from Westerham, the 07.07, would reach Charing Cross at 08.19. In

▲ Thanks to the railway, Westerham attracted many walkers and cyclists. This Edwardian postcard shows one of the steep hills rising into the woodlands to the south of Westerham. The cyclist shown here is enjoying the steep descent into the valley, while a horse-drawn wagon labours uphill.

COUNTRY AFTERNOON TICKETS

FROM LONDON AND SUBURBS

MARCH 26th to OCTOBER 29th inclusive 1961

▶ British Railways' Country Afternoon Tickets promoted outings to rural stations easily accessible from central London. The text sets the scene: 'No early morning rush. A lie-in, and then an easy run out when the day is nicely aired.' Westerham is included in this 1961 schedule, with tickets priced at 5s 3d return.

▶ ▶ A classic branch line scene on a summer's day in 1959, as an ancient push-pull unit drifts into Brasted station. Only one person waits on the platform, probably a friend of the photographer, not a passenger. The traditional timber station has plenty of period details, notably the South Eastern Railway lamp and the 1930s Southern Railway target-style, enamel name plaque.

its later years it was the commuters who kept the line running. While local freight was important, this was primarily a passenger line. For this reason, it was one of the first branches to have steam rail motors. These were introduced in April 1906 but were soon replaced with push-pull units, which became the standard vehicles on the line for the rest of its life. Towards the end, as on so many branch lines, these units were positively antiquated.

Closure, which came quickly, in October 1961, was partly for political reasons, as the trackbed was required for the route of the proposed London orbital motorway (M25) and the Sevenoaks bypass. It was the building of these roads that prevented an active and well-supported preservation group, which revived the old name, the Westerham Valley Railway, from saving or restoring the line. After closure, the remains of the line lingered on for some years until the new roads were built, at which point most of the route was completely obliterated.

▲ Westerham station, seen here near the end of the line's life, was the archetypal branch line terminus, with a small engine shed, signal box, goods yard, sidings, loading gauge and water tower – plus a delightful sense of leisurely inactivity. The push-pull unit simmers in the platform, having arrived on one of its many journeys from the junction at Dunton Green. No passengers seem to be arriving or departing; in fact, there is no one to be seen at all on this lazy summer's day.

Lost to the motorway

The Westerham branch traversed the pleasant valley of the Darenth, at this point little more than a stream, running parallel to the Pilgrim's Way in the shadow of the North Downs. The route was predominantly rural, and the intermediate stops at Brasted and Chevening Halt were well away from the settlements they served. To the south lay the wooded expanses of Hosey Hill and Brasted Chart, an area whose many roads and tracks were popular with walkers and cyclists. Chartwell, home of Sir Winston Churchill, is at the heart of this hilly and secluded landscape.

Finding traces of the railway today is quite hard. Westerham station has been completely redeveloped, and the line survives only in local road names, such as The Flyer's Way. The few remains that are to be found are mostly just to the west of the junction at Dunton Green, an area away from the motorway's route. At Dunton Green itself, the bay platform from which the Westerham trains departed can still be identified amid the overgrowth.

► In the 1940s the White Hart became one of the best-known pubs in southern England because of its popularity with fighter pilots stationed at Biggin Hill. It was famous for a blackboard, made from an old black-out panel, that was signed by many of the great names of the Battle of Britain. The pilots raced down from the airfield in cars, and probably never used the railway station. The blackboard is now in a local museum.

▼ Very little of the Westerham branch remains as most of the route is now under the M25. However, a wooded section survives to the east of Dunton Green, marked by a dense line of trees along the edge of a meadow, seen here filled with the soft greens of spring.

"THE PEW", WHITE HART HOTEL, BRASTED, KENT.

WHITE HART HOTEL, BRASTED, KENT

Paddock Wood to Hawkhurst

Born, like so many minor Victorian railways, out of intercompany rivalry, the Hawkhurst branch was a classic of its type. Single tracked and steam worked through its life, it ran through lovely countryside from nowhere to nowhere in particular, calling at stations that were generally a long way from the villages they claimed to serve.

▲ Old railways survive most often as tracks used by farmers. This example is on the former Hawkhurst branch.

The branch was opened in September 1892, having been built by the South Eastern Railway mainly to keep their rival, the London, Chatham & Dover, out of their territory. For decades it slumbered on, passing in due time into the care of the Southern Railway and thence to British Railways.

A red-letter day in Goudhurst in September 1892 with the arrival of the first train, greeted by a large and entirely male crowd, notable for the range of heights and the variety of headgear. The South Eastern Railway's locomotive, elaborately garlanded, was already a bit long in the tooth, setting the standard for the branch throughout its life. The carriages also seem to be a mixed lot. The station was then called Hope Mill, an acknowledgement that it was a long way from Goudhurst.

Goudhurst

► A classic branch line scene at Hawkhurst, shortly before the line's closure in 1961. It is the British Railways era, yet the station and its lamp are pure South Eastern Railway, while the station name board and the push-pull unit date from pre-war Southern days. The driver watches his passengers assemble on a grey day in the late 1950s. Most of them, including the smartly dressed lady, seem to be off to London for the day. The man looking at the camera has the air of a railway enthusiast; he and his friend, taking the photograph, are perhaps on a branch line tour.

◄ Looking out of place in the rail-less environment of an industrial estate, Hawkhurst's preserved signal box is nevertheless carefully painted and named in classic Southern Railway style. This is the site of Hawkhurst's former station, which, like most on the branch, was a long way from the place it was designed to serve. Other railway survivors include the old goods shed and the old engine shed, conveniently labelled for easy identification.

London Bridge to the branch line's stations via meandering routes. When the mechanization of hop picking brought these to an end in the 1950s, the line was doomed.

Towards the end of its life there was even a scheme to electrify it, in the hope of building commuter traffic, but it amounted to nothing and closure came in June 1961.

Ironically, today it would have been a valuable and busy commuter line. There was freight traffic, but more significant, and a defining characteristic of the branch, were the annual hop-pickers' specials, long trains of ancient carriages hauled by equally elderly locomotives that made their way from

Although much of the trackbed is still there in the rolling Kent countryside, it is hard to see today because most of the route is rural and away from roads. The bits that can be seen are private. Bridges have gone, along with most of the stations. Some of the tall, grand station houses survive, for example at Horsmonden, and at Hawkhurst there are engine and goods sheds, and a preserved signal box.

Chippenham to Calne

The Calne Railway opened its five and a bit miles of branch line from Chippenham in November 1863. Originally broad gauge, it was converted to standard gauge in the 1870s by the Great Western, who took over the branch completely in 1892.

Station Road, Calne

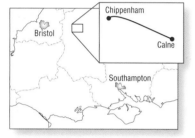

It was a line that had its own character, meandering prettily along the valley of the River Marden with two intermediate halts that appeared to serve nowhere in particular, Stanley Bridge and Black Dog. The latter was decidedly eccentric. It was built for the Marquis of Landsdowne, whose family estate at Bowood lies just to the south. In effect Black Dog was a private station (it did not appear in timetables until 1952) but it nevertheless boasted a waiting room, ticket office, siding and station master, a position subsequently reduced to leading porter. It seems the marquis insisted that the appointment of the station master was dependent upon his having no political views. As late as the 1960s, intending passengers at Black Dog halt were required to 'inform the guard' or 'give the necessary hand signal to the driver'. For many years the mainstay of the line was Calne's major industry, Harris & Company's manufacturing of sausage, pie and meat products. Towards the end of the line's life, sausages were regularly transported in passenger trains, a

▲ 'Station Road, Calne' is the title of this Edwardian postcard, issued by a local publisher. Children watch as sheep are driven along the road in a somewhat desultory manner on a lazy summer's afternoon.

G.W.R.

Calne

▶ Calne was a typical branch line terminus, with some freight sidings and a single platform covered by a generous canopy. The line was never busy, so the scene below, with nothing much going on, must have been very typical. The railings have just been painted, and a carriage waits at the far end of the platform. Today, the station site is an industrial estate.

practice that continued until the branch closed in September 1964.

The line has now been given a new lease of life by the sustainable transport charity Sustrans, as part of the National Cycle Network's Severn and Thames Route. Exploration is therefore easy and pleasant for both cyclists and walkers. The surface is good, access is well marked by typical Sustrans sculptures, and there is the excitement of a fine timber bridge across the A4 outside Calne. There is not much to see in Calne itself, but the trackbed wanders delightfully through green and undulating farmland interspersed with woods. Beyond Stanley Bridge it goes straight across the low-lying fields to Chippenham.

▼ Calne's major employer, and a prime user of the railway, was Harris & Company, meat purveyors and manufacturers of meat products. For years, Harris's pies were famous across Britain. This card, showing a very different view of Station Road from the rural scene above, makes clear the size of the factory. Today, both factory and station have gone.

CLN 2   CALNE, VIEW FROM STATION ROAD.

▲ The Calne branch survives today as a well-surfaced and pleasant path through the countryside, popular with both walkers and cyclists. Part of the National Cycle Network's Thames and Severn route, it is a typical Sustrans track, with sculptural route markers and a dramatic new bridge over the A4 road.

The Isle of Wight

The island's distinctive character was created by the Victorians, and the survival of this today is part of the appeal of a place that seems to encompass the best features of Britain's past. The comprehensive railway system, built between 1862 and 1900 by a series of fiercely independent local companies, was the key to its development.

SOUTHERN RAILWAY.
(2/37)   (787 G)
FROM WATERLOO TO
BRADING
Via PORTSMOUTH.

▲ Complete with a border of embossed shells, this postcard captures the flavour of the Isle of Wight during the nineteenth century. Having seduced Queen Victoria, Prince Albert and Lord Tennyson, the island became a popular and fashionable place to visit from the 1850s. Seaside holidays, rural retreats and souvenirs were all part of the picture, and exploration was made easy by the railway and the bicycle.

▼ The last railway to be opened on the island ran from Newport to Ventnor via Godshill. It was also one of the first to be closed. Here, on 26 July 1897, a surprisingly small group stands by the inaugural train, which is lavishly adorned with flags and greenery. The opening of a railway was still something to celebrate at the very end of Queen Victoria's reign.

▶ Ryde's new railway pier was completed in 1880, enabling passengers to walk straight from the steamer on to one of the trains that ran to many parts of the island. Miraculously, this can still be done today, although the train goes only to Shanklin. Previously, there was a tramway service along the pier, to carry passengers from the ferry to Ryde's town station.

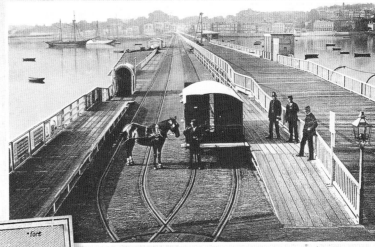

The companies merged into two railways, the Isle of Wight and the Isle of Wight Central. In 1923 the network became part of the Southern Railway, and, later, of British Railways, but nothing much changed.

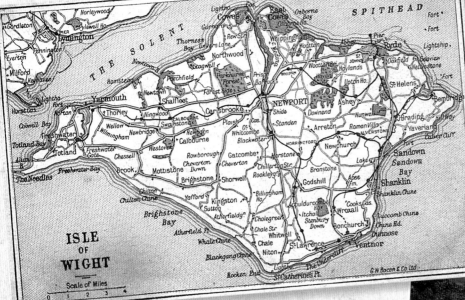

ISLE
OF
WIGHT

Scale of Miles

◀ The complete Isle of Wight railway system can be seen on this 1930s map. Newport was the hub of the network, and from here lines radiated west to Yarmouth and Freshwater, north to Cowes, east to Ryde, Bembridge, Sandown and Shanklin, and south to Ventnor, via two routes. This series of interconnected branch lines made island exploration very easy.

▼ The seaside and the varied beaches made the Isle of Wight a very popular choice for family holidays from the late Victorian era. This postcard, showing a fine array of beach tents, was sent from Shanklin in July 1920. The message, to a neighbour in Harrow-on-the-Hill, Middlesex, says: 'Returning on Saturday, will you please take two loaves for me.' The weather had, apparently, been unsettled.

Until the early 1950s the entire island was criss-crossed by what were, in effect, Victorian branch lines. Sadly, closures broke the pattern and by the mid-1960s all had gone except the line from Ryde Pierhead to Shanklin. Electrified in 1967, this has been operated for many years by retired London tube trains, an eccentricity that underlines the island's particular quality.

Bathing Beach, Small Hope, Shanklin, I.W.

The island's most remarkable station was Ventnor, built in 1866 on the site of a former quarry and approached directly from a long tunnel under St Boniface Down. This was a busy place, and the railway was Ventnor's lifeline over a long period. As can be seen in this 1960 photograph, the railway, even then, carried plenty of freight, notably coal and other basic commodities.

A popular place for rail enthusiasts was the Medina bridge at Newport, and the scene shown was captured by many photographers. Here a train from Cowes to Ryde crosses the bridge in the 1950s, hauled by one of the island's distinctive tank locomotives. Some of these remained in service right up to the closure of the network in 1966. Cars complete the period look.

Despite the expansion of private motoring in the 1950s and early 1960s, the railways were still a major part of the island's economy. This view of the front of Ventnor station shows an interesting range of cars old and new. Their owners were no doubt meeting friends and relatives newly arrived from Ryde or Cowes.

Southern England: The Isle of Wight

► In August 1953 a young boy called David sent this card to his Sunday School teacher, declaring in big letters: 'I am having a good holiday.' The theme, the slowness of local trains, was a popular one from the early years of the twentieth century. This scene of the railway staff playing cricket while the passengers wait was widely available, overprinted with the names of many places where the train service was considered to be erratic.

▼ The least-used part of the island's network was the line from Merstone Junction south to Ventnor West. It was completed in 1900 by the Newport, Godshill & St Lawrence Railway. It soon went bankrupt, and was finally closed in 1953. This 1930s view of Whitwell station shows the rural nature of this remote railway. The man on the platform may have a long wait.

▲ The old route of the railway from Yarmouth station – which survives, with its platform – to the outskirts of Freshwater has long been a footpath, cycleway and occasional bridleway. This wooded section is at the Freshwater end.

◄ In December 1966, right at the end of the Isle of Wight's railway network, a classic branch line scene takes place as the driver of the Ryde to Shanklin train reaches out to take the single-line token from the signalman at Ryde St John's Road.

[49]

Longmoor Military Railway

The Victorian army appreciated the strategic value of railways. Engineers, for example, were given specialist training in railway work for the Sudan and Egyptian campaigns.

Training carried on at Woolwich Arsenal and elsewhere until 1905, when the Woolmer Instructional Military Railway was set up in Hampshire to train military engineers in all aspects of railway construction, operation and management. In 1935 this became the Longmoor Military Railway. Running from a branch from Bentley, near Alton, to Liss on the Petersfield line, this was a complete railway network, serving camps, firing ranges, training areas, workshops and depots. There were thirteen intermediate stations and miles of sidings, many of which were vital in the build-up to D-Day in 1944. In later years Longmoor was famous for its annual open day. The railway closed in 1969 and today there is little to be seen, with much of the route still on army land. The southern section is a footpath, the Royal Woolmer Way.

▶ Finding the remains of the Longmoor Railway is hard as much is still on army land. Hidden in the woods near Bordon are concrete buffers, the remains of long sidings where trains were hidden prior to D-Day.

▲ Bordon Camp was a massive military base, served by the Longmoor Railway and by the LSWR branch from Bentley (closed to passengers in 1957). This card shows the Wesleyan Soldiers' Home at Bordon, c.1910.

▲ Longmoor Camp itself is to the south of Bordon. The route of the old line towards Longmoor is popular with walkers and cyclists.

▶ Longmoor open days were popular events each year, with trains from the railway's unusual fleet on show, including 'Gordon', the famous WD 2-10-0 locomotive. This shows an early 1960s open day.

LONGMOOR MILITARY RAILWAY
OPEN DAY - 3rd JUNE, 1967
Valid for travel between LISS,
LONGMOOR DOWNS & OaKHANGER
and via HOLLYWATER LOOP
For conditions see over
Williamson, Ticket Printer, Ashton-u-Lyne
0621   0621

◀ The most accessible part of the former railway today is the section north of Liss, part of which is now the Royal Woolmer Way. Among the surviving relics to be seen is this bridge over a stream, dramatically hidden in woods, and clearly built to carry heavy trains.

East Anglia

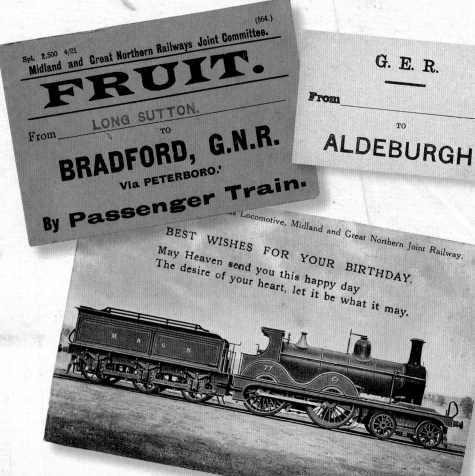

G. E. R.

From

TO

ALDEBURGH

ss Locomotive, Midland and Great Northern Joint Railway.

BEST WISHES FOR YOUR BIRTHDAY.
May Heaven send you this happy day
The desire of your heart, let it be what it may.

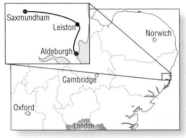

Saxmundham to Aldeburgh

In the mid-nineteenth century, independent companies were building railways all over East Anglia. Two that were particularly active in Suffolk were the Eastern Counties and the East Suffolk, whose branch lines to Framlingham, Leiston and Snape were opened on 1 June 1859.

Aldeburgh, South Parade.

The following year the branch from Saxmundham to Leiston was extended to Aldeburgh. Later, all these came under the control of the Great Eastern Railway. This ambitious company, which was subsequently absorbed into the LNER, was keen to develop holiday traffic in East Anglia, so excursions and through trains were run from London to Aldeburgh until 1939. To make the most of this traffic, Aldeburgh was given a smart station with a train shed and a long, single platform.

A resort since the early nineteenth century, Aldeburgh was famous for its Georgian terraces, fishermen's cottages, wide shingle beach and, above all, for its old-fashioned air of traditional seaside elegance. The railway contributed further to the town's popularity. Also important in railway terms was the development of Thorpeness, a holiday village built from scratch before World War I with a range of houses in a variety of styles, a large lake and a golf course. Naturally Thorpeness acquired a station, but it was a long way from the village, the railway's route at that point being well inland. Despite the continuing popularity of these resorts, the opening of the opera house at nearby Snape in 1948 and the continuing presence of a large engineering works with its own rail yard at Leiston, traffic on the Aldeburgh line declined steadily through the 1950s and 1960s, and closure came in September 1966.

◀ In 1909, when this postcard was sent, Aldeburgh was a popular but undeveloped resort whose beach was evidently still used, for the most part, by local fishermen rather than by the visitors who are here seen ambling along South Parade.

G. E. R.

From

TO

ALDEBURGH

▲ In June 1963 a two-coach, diesel railcar waits at Aldeburgh for the few passengers still using the railway. Freight traffic had stopped in 1959, and a crane is at work demolishing the remains of the goods yard.

◀ Aldeburgh station in the 1950s was a busy place, judging by the neatly lined up barrows. However, not many people have arrived on the train from Saxmundham, so there is plenty of time for staff to chat.

Servicing the energy industry

Although it is now closed to passenger traffic, the Aldeburgh branch has been maintained as far as Leiston for the nuclear flask traffic for the Sizewell power stations, the first of which opened in 1966. Currently this amounts to an average of one train a week. As the track and infrastructure are still intact, including old-fashioned hand-operated level crossings with wooden gates, it is easy to follow this part of the route on nearby minor roads. With so much still in place, and yet with the atmosphere of a branch line of the past, there is a kind of *Marie Celeste* feeling about the line.

For example, Leiston station has a platform and sidings, and the remains of station lamps, but the building itself is a private house and there are no passengers.

From Leiston south to Aldeburgh, things are much harder. There is not much to see of the line as it runs across farmland and then over the coastal heathland. Much of the route is inaccessible, but part of it is now a nature reserve. Visible but overgrown is the platform of Thorpeness's remote station, barely noticed by the passing golfers. Long gone are the old coach bodies that used to serve as station buildings, and in Aldeburgh itself there is little to see in railway terms.

▶ On the part of the line that is kept open for the nuclear flask trains, nothing much has changed since the 1960s. There are plenty of survivals as a result, including this manually operated gate at a level crossing.

▲ Keen eyes may spot the concrete platform of Thorpeness station hidden in the undergrowth beside the golf course. The station was opened in the Edwardian era to serve the rapidly expanding, but rather distant, holiday village on the coast.

► At Leiston the rails are bright and the platform is complete but overgrown. At the time of writing, about one train a week passes through and it does not stop for passengers. The station buildings are now a private house. Beyond the crossing, the line continues as far as the loading bay for the Sizewell nuclear flask trains, just outside Leiston.

▲ In the evening light, the station lamps should be coming on, but this one at Leiston has not been lit for forty years. Yet it is still there, along with the bracket that carried the totem name plate, now on display in some enthusiast's collection, perhaps.

► Before the power stations came, the major industry on the branch was Richard Garrett of Leiston, engineers and makers of all kinds of steam engines. The large factory had its own railway connection, as is shown here in this remarkable, pre-World War I photograph of the staff pouring out for their tea break.

Kelvedon to Tollesbury

The grandly named Kelvedon, Tiptree & Tollesbury Pier Light Railway was a typical creation of the 1896 Light Railways Act, and thus authorized in 1901. The first 9 miles were slowly built through rural Essex to the estuary of the River Blackwater and finally opened in October 1904.

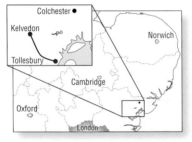

Three years later, the line was extended to Tollesbury pier. Cheaply built and operated, the railway featured stations with low platforms, no signalling to speak of, and a variety of ancient rolling stock acquired second or third hand. Tickets were issued on the trains. Run somewhat reluctantly by the Great Eastern Railway, it was at first successful, transporting jam, from Wilkinson's Tiptree factory, and prodigious amounts of shellfish harvested by the local fishing fleets. It is recorded that on one day the railway carried 110,000 oysters from Tollesbury to Kelvedon. It was this fish traffic that gave rise to the line's popular name, the 'crab and winkle'. However, the real hopes for the line, based on expanded use of Tollesbury pier, never materialized, partly because silting of the estuary made the pier inaccessible to ships of any size. The 1920s saw the end of traffic to the pier, which then quietly decayed until the floods of 1953 swept it all away. On the rest of the line, traffic was maintained through the LNER era and into the early years of British

▲ In the autumn of 1949 two enthusiasts pose with the guard for a photograph in one of the line's bogie coaches, a vehicle used formerly on the Wisbech & Upwell tramway. They seem to be looking forward to a journey that was by then a relatively rare experience, for the railway saw few passengers in the last years of its life.

▼ At Kelvedon there were two stations, linked by a spur line. One was on the main line and the other, for the Tollesbury Railway, was on a lower level. Changing trains was, therefore, never straightforward. This 1948 photograph shows the light railway's Kelvedon station, where a train has just arrived from Tollesbury.

Railways, but by 1951 everyone had had enough, and passenger services were withdrawn. For some years, freight services were maintained as far as Tiptree, mostly for the jam factory, but these ended in October 1962. Since then the railway has all but vanished. Sold off piecemeal, the trackbed has mostly been ploughed out, and only a filled-in bridge, short stretches of low embankment and the occasional Station Road in a rural village reveal that there ever was a railway to Tollesbury.

▲ Built cheaply across a flat landscape and mostly closed half a century ago, the Tollesbury branch has left few traces. Nearly all the trackbed has been ploughed back into the fields from which it came. A rare survival is a short stretch near Tolleshunt D'Arcy, a village in which there is a Station Road but no sign of a station.

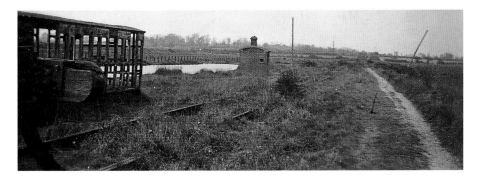

▲ Having never fulfilled its promise, the extension to Tollesbury pier was abandoned in the 1920s. It was then left to its own devices, overgrown and quietly decaying, until the remains were swept away in the 1953 floods. Today there is little to indicate that Tollesbury ever had a railway.

▼ The Tollesbury branch was well known for the random and often ramshackle nature of its rolling stock. This is apparent in this mixed-stock train in the 1950s, hauled by an old North Eastern Railway tank locomotive still in LNER colours.

Spalding to Yarmouth

In the 1850s and 1860s East Anglia was a bit of a railway battlefield, keenly fought over by a series of ambitious companies, notably East Anglian Railways, the Eastern Counties Railway and the Eastern Union Railway.

THE BRITANNIA PIER, GT YARMOUTH

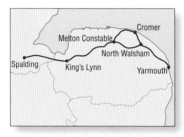

Larger companies, including the Great Northern or the Midland, were frequently lurking in the background, while in the foreground was a plethora of little local companies, often the pawns in the battle. Among these were the Lynn & Dereham, the Lynn & Fakenham, the Lynn & Sutton Bridge, the Norwich & Spalding, the Wells & Fakenham, the Yarmouth & North Norfolk and the Yarmouth & Norwich. Things became a bit clearer after 1862, with the formation of the Great Eastern Railway, which took over much of the network. Exceptions were the routes across north Norfolk, but many of these came together in 1883 as the Eastern & Midlands Railway. The geographical centre of the network was Melton Constable, a remote village where the Lynn & Fakenham company, now part of the Eastern & Midlands, had chosen to place its railway works. This remained the status quo for

▼ This Edwardian view of Sheringham's High Street has plenty of period detail, conveying the style and atmosphere of this smart little seaside resort largely created by the M&GNJR. Sheringham's elegant station is still in use, by the preserved North Norfolk Railway, and the town is connected to the national network via a branch from Norwich.

▲ This card of Yarmouth's Britannia Pier was posted in 1906, at the peak of the development of this Norfolk coast resort. The railways played a crucial role in that process, and celebrated that by producing promotional postcards. Yarmouth Beach station was the starting point for many a holiday visit.

High Street, Sheringham

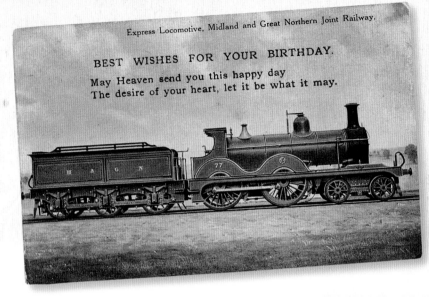

Express Locomotive, Midland and Great Northern Joint Railway.

BEST WISHES FOR YOUR BIRTHDAY.

May Heaven send you this happy day
The desire of your heart, let it be what it may.

◀ The M&GNJR's locomotives of the
1890s were noted for their elegance
of line and attractive colour scheme,
both of which are well shown on this
Edwardian birthday card.

▼ On a summer Sunday in 1958 a long holiday train en route from Spalding to
Hunstanton pauses at the tiny station of Gedney, west of Sutton Bridge. Little
stations such as this, serving remote communities, were a feature of the line.

In the late 1950s a long holiday special, double-headed by two LMS freight locomotives, comes slowly into Sutton Bridge station. Much of the M&GNJR's 182-mile network was single-tracked, with passing places at the stations.

ten years, but the big players, the Midland and the Great Northern, were still keen to be involved, particularly if by so doing they could thwart the Great Eastern. So they formed in 1893 the Midland & Great Northern Joint Railway, to take over the interests of the Eastern & Midland and some other bits and pieces. This resulted in an independent 182-mile network, spreading from Spalding, Peterborough and King's Lynn in the west to Cromer, Yarmouth and Lowestoft in the east, with a branch to Norwich in the centre. Much of it was a classic rural railway, serving small communities and local needs, but it was able to benefit from expanding holiday traffic to east coast resorts and useful freight connections with other networks. During its lifetime, the M&GNJR maintained a spirit of independence and its smart, light-brown coloured locomotives continued to run until 1923, when it was all absorbed into the LNER. Even then, its local

Spl. 2,500 4/21   (564.)

Midland and Great Northern Railways Joint Committee.

FRUIT.

From   LONG SUTTON.

TO

BRADFORD, G.N.R.

Via PETERBORO.'

By Passenger Train.

character endured, and continued to do so into the era of British Railways. However, by the 1950s the death knell was tolling for this type of rural network. In many of the areas it served, road transport was cheaper and quicker. So closures began. By the end of the 1960s the M&GNJR had in effect ceased to exist, although some freight services lingered on until the 1980s. Today a short stretch from Cromer to Sheringham is the only bit to survive as part of the national network. A more significant survival, or rather revival, is the North Norfolk's preserved line from Sheringham to Holt.

▼ The M&GNJR's station for King's Lynn was South Lynn, close to the crossing of the Great Ouse on the iron girder bridge shown here. In 1958 a long train hauled, no doubt with some difficulty, by an old LMS freight locomotive passes the distinctive M&GN somersault signals.

The route today

The flat landscape of the Wash offered few challenges to Victorian railway engineers, other than a number of crossings over various waterways. The line's original builders were generous with stations in the empty landscape east of Spalding. Often they served minute communities such as Fleet, Gedney, Walpole and Terrington, some of which lay a distance from the railway. The route from Spalding is remote, but the remains can be followed from minor roads, which regularly cross the trackbed. At Sutton Bridge, which is the first major river crossing, the M&GNJR built a large girder bridge with an opening span. This bridge was shared with a

▼ In 1962 Melton Constable still had a substantial station. In many ways it was the heart of the M&GNJR network, with lines radiating in four directions. Today everything has gone, and it is hard to believe the town ever had a railway station, let alone a major railway workshop.

▲ Much of the extensive network of the M&GNJR has vanished, but in the low-lying landscape those bits that remain are easily spotted. This long embankment across the ploughed fields of early spring is near Corpusty, between Melton Constable and Aylsham.

road and when the railway closed in 1959 the road took it over completely, along with a section of the trackbed to the east. The next major structure was the bridge across the Great Ouse, south of King's Lynn, but this has gone. For a while, the section east of Lynn remained in use as a freight line but this too closed years ago.

The line from Lynn to Fakenham was equally rural and remote, and maintained the pattern of serving small places a long way from the railway. Sections have disappeared but there is still plenty for the diligent explorer to find in the landscape. At Fakenham the M&GNJR had its own station, well to the west but called Fakenham Town regardless. The line crossed the Great Eastern's route northwards

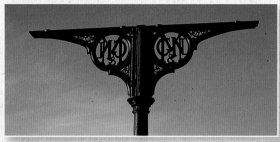

◄ Cromer Beach station was opened in 1887 and brought the resort to life. The M&GNJR made the most of this smart station, which at the time of this photograph was the eastern terminus of their network. Today the buildings survive, in other uses, and trains still come to Cromer station.

▲ Iron pillars decorated with the initials of the companies that built Yarmouth Beach station now stand in a car park as a kind of memorial to a station of which there is today no other trace. This one commemorates the Midland & Great Northern.

to Wells and then meandered through a more rounded and wooded landscape to Melton Constable. Of the great railway works that were constructed here, in the empty Norfolk landscape, from 1882, remarkably little remains; just a few indeterminate buildings, a massive water tower and some meaningless bits and pieces scattered around a little town whose raison d'être has vanished.

Melton was also a meeting point of four lines, west to Fakenham, east to Aylsham, south to Norwich and north to Cromer. The routes to Norwich and Aylsham are best preserved, with embankments, bridges and stations to be seen, but little remains of the route towards Cromer until just outside Holt, where it all suddenly comes back to life. A station, track and trains indicate the thriving presence of the preserved North Norfolk Railway, and in its care the memory of the M&GNJR lives on. At Sheringham the preserved railway meets the real thing which by comparison

seems mean and minimal. Next comes Cromer, and more complicated history, involving three railway companies and two stations. The survivor is what was originally called Cromer Beach, an 1887 timber-framed Arts & Crafts-style building. It was this station that began the development of Cromer into a select Edwardian resort, echoes of which can be faintly detected. From Cromer there were two other routes, direct to Norwich on the Great Eastern, or a meander along the coast in the trains of the Norfolk & Suffolk Joint Railway, which arrived in 1906. These two met at North Walsham, a busy railway junction in its heyday and still a living station on the Sheringham line.

To the west, the M&GNJR's line towards Aylsham is now defined as a footpath called the Weavers' Way. This continues to the east of North Walsham, with the footpath rejoining the railway north of Horning for a short stretch. This is a good section, with woods and waterways all around, and then

it disappears into the landscape and beneath a road. From here into Yarmouth, much of the trackbed has been returned to the fields from which it came. A big bridge survives at Hemsby, now carrying a road over nothing, and a few other traces can be found. However, gone for ever are the big holiday expresses sweeping along the coast, through the suburbs and into Yarmouth Beach station, a grand terminus suitable for the resort that Yarmouth then was. Today, nothing remains of this but a few cast-iron pillars used to decorate a car park.

▲ In the 1950s much of the network was still intact and busy with both expresses and local services. This is the stopping train from Yarmouth Beach to North Walsham, seen here departing from Caister-on-Sea, a station virtually on the beach and famous for its holiday camps.

▶ A surprising survivor is this bridge plate, set into the stonework of a busy road bridge near Hemsby. The trackbed that ran beneath it and across the surrounding fields having been obliterated, the bridge now carries the traffic over nothing.

Peterborough to King's Lynn

The low-lying landscape of Lincolnshire and north Cambridgeshire encouraged the building of railways and, until the 1960s, a dense network served the region.

MURROW. MID. & G.N. STATION.

Some duplication was inevitable; typical were the two routes from Peterborough to Wisbech and King's Lynn. The more direct was a line completed in 1866, linking Peterborough and Sutton Bridge via Wisbech. At Sutton Bridge it met the line to King's Lynn, while from Wisbech there was another, older route via Watlington (or Magdalen Road, as it became), built originally as a branch by the Lynn & Ely Railway. Mergers brought the two routes into different ownership but all became part of the LNER and then British Railways, until closure in the 1960s. The landscape that made the railways easy to build also made them easy to remove, with the result that today there is little to be seen. The trackbed is visible in places, for example east of Peterborough, but has largely been ploughed out. Stations do survive, with

▲ At Murrow the line to Wisbech crossed the line from March to Spalding on the level and there were two stations, West and East. This is East, on the Wisbech line. Today, traces of the former junction can be seen, including a goods shed.

Train Leaving G. E. Station, Peterboro'. P.S.

▶ Peterborough had several stations but the starting point for this route was Peterborough East, shown in this Edwardian postcard with a train ready to depart.

The Steam Tram, Elm Road, Wisbech.

◄ Wisbech had a complicated railway history, with three stations, serving three lines, and the little steam tramway to Upwell, seen here in about 1910 at the start of its line, by Wisbech East station.

▼ The stations between Wisbech and King's Lynn on the former branch from Watlington were quite distinctive, as this 1920s view of Emneth shows. Note the old carriage body behind the platform, probably used as a store.

▼ Remarkably, several stations on the Wisbech-to-Watlington section survive as private houses, though the track has generally vanished. This is Emneth. The carriage parked in the garden echoes the old photograph alongside.

▲ Much of the former route from Wisbech towards Sutton Bridge can be walked, with the wide Nene flowing beyond the embankment on the right. This is the view along the trackbed towards the remarkably remote Ferry station, now a private house.

◄ The line had few engineering features and most were removed long ago. Two large bridges do survive, rather unexpectedly, though with no trackbed to connect them. This one crosses the Middle Level Main Drain. From the other, across the Hundred Foot Drain, the old embankment curved away towards Watlington.

▼ The vast majority of the trackbed has simply been ploughed back into the fields but traces do remain. This old concrete bridge over a stream survives near Smeeth Road, completely isolated and surrounded by fields of cabbages and other crops.

Ferry, Tydd, Emneth, Smeeth Road and Middle Drove all recognizable, but mostly now private houses. The section from Wisbech to Sutton Bridge is a footpath along the Nene, but nothing else can really be walked. However, the dedicated explorer will find other traces, notably bridges, a couple of which are surprisingly substantial survivors.

▶ A busy port and major railway centre until the 1960s, King's Lynn was, and still is, a town with a great architectural heritage, as this 1950s card of the Old Customs House shows.

▼ Watlington, or Magdalen Road as it was from the 1870s, is still a station on the main line from Cambridge to King's Lynn. It looks not unlike this 1950s photograph. The old junction with the Wisbech line was to the south of the station.

Mid-Suffolk Light Railway

Railway fever gripped Britain in the first half of the nineteenth century. There were triumphs and disasters but much of the national network was built relatively quickly. By the 1880s most things were in place though minor additions continued to be made.

However, the passing of the Light Railways Act in 1896 gave a new impetus to railway building, particularly in rural areas. Light railways did not need crossing gates, complex signalling or even platforms, but speeds were limited to 25mph. Typical of those built under the Act was the Mid-Suffolk Light Railway, whose planned line between Haughley and Halesworth, on the Lowestoft line via Beccles, with a long branch south to Westerfield, near Ipswich, was approved in 1901. With great ceremony, the first sod was cut at Westerfield on 3 May 1902, though the railway was destined never to get that far. In 1904 the section between Haughley East and Laxfield was opened by a company with strong local support and its own locomotives. Money problems soon affected the line and brought work to a standstill in 1907. At that point, the main line had continued for a couple of miles beyond Laxfield to Cratfield, while the branch had reached Debenham. The railway, designed to serve a remote part of Suffolk, had depended on its connections with other lines, none of which were to be realized. It became instead a rural branch line serving nowhere in particular. Somehow it survived as

▶ From Haughley there were nine stations, all serving small places and built in a rather rudimentary way from corrugated iron. This gave the line a distinctive look. This is Mendlesham, probably in the 1930s. Note the decorative iron lettering on the nameboard. All to be seen today is a street named Old Station Road.

[72]

◄ The exploration of old railways, even ones that have gone almost without trace, can still spring surprises. This former GER carriage, which may have run on the Mid-Suffolk line, stands abandoned in a field near Mendlesham. Formerly used as a cottage, it is now clearly on its last legs.

► The supports of an old bridge and a tall embankment mark the route of the line as it swung away from Haughley East, at the start of its 19-mile journey to nowhere.

▲ The Mid-Suffolk Light Railway was cheaply built across farmland, so it was quickly and easily returned to that farmland after it closed. As a result, few stretches of identifiable trackbed remain, making its route hard to follow. A good place is the site of Aspall & Thorndon station, typically one that served nowhere in particular, not even a village. Yet the site survives, along with something that may have been a platform. Across the road the trackbed sets off through the trees. It does not look like a railway but in Mid-Suffolk terms this is a major survivor.

◄ The Mid-Suffolk closed in 1952 and much of it quickly disappeared. However, some things did survive for a surprisingly long time. This is Horham station in 1977, under inspection by a smartly dressed young man, wearing the flared trousers of that era. He is clearly not the typical railway enthusiast.

an independent company until absorbed by the LNER in 1924. By the late 1940s there were two trains a day, usually mixed passenger and freight, so no one was surprised when passenger services ceased in 1952.

Lightly constructed and with no engineering features of note, the line has now largely vanished back into the Suffolk farmland. However, there are things to be seen, including the remains of bridges near Haughley and a section of trackbed used as a footpath west of Mendlesham. Other short bits of the trackbed can be seen occasionally from minor roads, but it is impossible to trace the route in any conventional sense and it has mostly disappeared from the Ordnance Survey map. All that remains in Mendlesham is a sign saying Old Station Road, but the site of Aspall & Thorndon station is still identifiable, as are some bridge supports and a section of embankment on the branch near Debenham. West of Laxfield there is the site of a crossing, with the keeper's cottage, and from here the trackbed, no more than a farm track, swings across the fields towards the village. At Brockford & Wetheringsett the Mid-Suffolk Light Railway comes briefly back to life, with a rebuilt and fully restored station and other buildings, a museum and a few hundred yards of relaid track. Trains do run and there is a collection of mainly Great Eastern Railway rolling stock.

◀ Laxfield is today a quiet rural village and in 1919, when this card was sent, it was even more so. Sadly, the highlights depicted here do not include the railway station.

Central England

G.E.R.
From IPSWICH SP
TO
HORNCASTLE
via G.N. & G.E. Joint Line
and Spalding.

Wantage Tramway

The Great Western Railway's line was built well to the north of Wantage, leaving the town without a railway. The GWR opened a station called Wantage Road, 'Road' being a nineteenth-century euphemism for a station miles from the town it claimed to serve. The citizens of Wantage were not satisfied and campaigned for a branch line. In 1875 the Wantage Tramway was opened.

Cheaply built, mostly along the edge of the main road, this basic railway was initially horse-drawn. Soon steam trams of various kinds arrived, and then in 1878 the company purchased the locomotive 'Shannon', which was destined to stay with the tramway throughout its existence. Once into its stride, the company operated an efficient service, meeting trains at Wantage Road and carrying ever-increasing amounts of freight, notably coal, corn, groceries and building materials. In 1905 nearly 55,000 passengers were carried in elaborate tramcar-like vehicles, and 5,000 wagons were moved up and down the line. Successful and profitable, the tramway even paid its shareholders a generous dividend. After World War I, however, everything changed. Road transport became more competitive, and in 1925 passenger carrying ended. Freight traffic continued, and the line remained in profit, albeit at the expense of track and vehicle maintenance. Everything came to an end on 21 December 1945, when the last train staggered along the by now almost impassable track. After closure, the remains of the tramway were quickly obliterated.

◄ More market town than tourist centre, Wantage none the less has had its fair share of postcards. This 1920s multi-view card shows some of the highlights, including the church of St Peter and St Paul, the school and the statue of King Alfred, born in the town in 849AD.

► The first proper locomotive on the line, and the best known, was No. 5, 'Shannon', an 0-4-0 built originally for the Sandy & Potton Railway. It arrived in 1878, and remained with the tramway until closure. This photograph of 'Shannon', accompanied by company staff, was taken in 1895. 'Shannon' survives, preserved at the Didcot Railway Centre.

▲ On a wet day in the 1930s, long after the abandonment of passenger carrying, the Wantage Tramway is still busy with freight. Locomotive No. 7, built in 1888, hauls a train of assorted box vans along the roadside line, a common sight until the 1940s.

◄ On 22 October 1873 a public meeting was called in Wantage under the chairmanship of Colonel Sir Robert Loyd Lindsay to campaign for a tramway link between the town and the GWR's main line, 2½ miles to the north. This led directly to the building of the tramway, which opened in October 1875. Always distinctive and full of character, the Wantage Tramway ran beside the road for much of its route. In its early days, it relied on steam tram engines, of the kind seen in the photograph.

[79]

Stonehouse to Nailsworth

Athough they were deep in GWR territory, Gloucester, Stroud and Bristol were also part of the Midland Railway's tentacle-like network. Indeed, the Midland had ambitious plans to invade Southampton via the Cotswolds, and the line to Nailsworth might have been the first stage of that assault.

▲ Railway rivalry gave Stroud two stations. The Midland Railway's branch to Stroud was an early closure to passengers in 1949. Goods traffic lingered on until 1 June 1966, shortly before this photograph was taken.

I n the event, all that was ever built was the short branch from Stonehouse, constructed by the independent and locally sponsored Stonehouse & Nailsworth Railway and opened in 1867. As was so often the case with these small companies, there was too much optimism and not enough money, so the railway was in financial difficulties within a few months of opening. The Midland Railway stepped in and a take-over was arranged in 1878. At the time, Stroud and Nailsworth, traditional wool towns, were major centres of textile production, and the railway seemed to be viable. In fact, freight did turn out to be significant, keeping the branch open until 1966. Passenger services had ended in June 1949, along with most of the old Midland Railway interests in the region, including their station at Stroud, Wallbridge. Long before Beeching, British Railways could see that running competing services over the same route was likely to be a waste of time, money and resources.

Nailsworth is a pleasant old town, squeezed into the meeting point of three steep river valleys. All that river water supplied power for the mills, but it also made access difficult. The branch line, therefore, was built close by the road that already ran along the narrow valley.

▼ In 1965 the regular pick-up goods train, hauled by a British Railways Standard locomotive, drifts past Ryecroft station. The platform has gone, the goods shed is abandoned and the whole station looks sad and run down. At this point there had been no passenger traffic for sixteen years, although a few enthusiasts' specials had penetrated the branch.

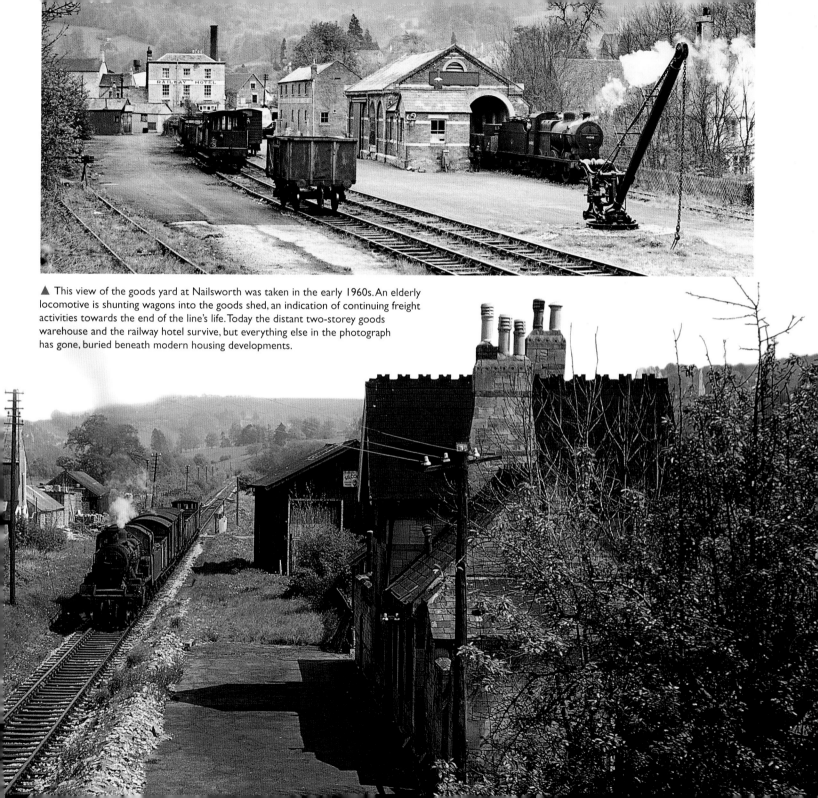

▲ This view of the goods yard at Nailsworth was taken in the early 1960s. An elderly locomotive is shunting wagons into the goods shed, an indication of continuing freight activities towards the end of the line's life. Today the distant two-storey goods warehouse and the railway hotel survive, but everything else in the photograph has gone, buried beneath modern housing developments.

▲ This photograph captures perfectly the atmosphere of a freight-only branch line near the end of its life. The grassy track, the hissing locomotive waiting while the fireman opens the old crossing gate, the abundance of encroaching nature and the little vegetable patch in the foreground with the beans growing well all add to the picture of a way of life gone for ever.

From railway track to cycle track

Today, the line is still there, converted into a cycle track. This offers an enjoyable and secluded route between Stonehouse and Nailsworth, shielded from the noisy road and the developing industrial and domestic buildings by woodland, which in spring is heavy with the scent of wild garlic. Although it was a short, relatively minor branch line, the railway builders invested in substantial stations, at Ryecroft, Dudbridge, Woodchester and Nailsworth. Of these, the most magnificent was at Nailsworth, a richly decorative High Victorian Gothic palace in local stone, with plenty of Cotswold details. Luckily, this survives. Along with its platform, it is in private hands but is easily appreciated from the cycle track and the surrounding roads. The building has many attractive features, notably the arched entrance arcade in Romanesque style, whose short columns and flowery capitals give it the look of a medieval cloister. The cycleway, well below the level of the station and platform, follows the old goods lines into what was a substantial goods yard. Here, a large brick warehouse survives, overlooked by a handsome stone building that is decoratively labelled Station Hotel. This goods yard was to have been the starting point for the Midland Railway's line southwards towards Southampton.

▶ 'Near Nailsworth, Glo'stershire': an artistic view of the wooded river valleys that meet at the town. Although the image is probably Edwardian, the card was posted in 1935. Today, parts of the cycleway along the route of the branch have a similar feeling, but cyclists are unlikely to encounter a milkmaid.

▼ An old LMS locomotive shunts the daily goods at Dudbridge in 1963. For nearly twenty years from 1949, the Nailsworth branch and the link to Stroud from Dudbridge were freight-only lines, and scenes such as this were commonplace. Dudbridge station is now a private house.

▼ Nailsworth station survives as a private house. This splendid stone-built structure in a kind of Cotswold Gothic style underlines the Victorian enthusiasm for even minor railways.

Near Nailsworth Glo'stershire.

Woodhall Junction to Horncastle

Many Victorian branch lines were local enterprises, built to satisfy the demands of the industry and business in the area and run with a degree of independence. The Horncastle Railway was just such an enterprise, set up in 1854 by local businessmen who wanted to link their town to the national network.

EAGLE LODGE HOTEL, WOODHALL SPA.

Initially they asked the Great Northern to build the line but, when that company refused, they went ahead and did it themselves. The 7-mile branch to the main line at Kirkstead (or Woodhall Junction, as it was later known) opened in 1855. Despite the pessimism of the Great Northern, which actually worked the line and took fifty per cent of the receipts, the railway regularly made a profit and the local shareholders regularly received dividends. Until 1915 there was even a through coach from London. Confronted with this unusual situation, the Great Northern naturally changed its tune and tried on several occasions up to 1920 to buy the company, but the Horncastle Railway remained independent until it was absorbed into the LNER in 1923.

The secret of the line's success was considerable freight traffic and the burgeoning popularity in the late Victorian period of Woodhall Spa as a resort. The exploitation of health-giving bromo-iodine waters (discovered by chance during a search for coal) and the rising enthusiasm for golf

◄ In February 1910 Mrs Mirrlees, no doubt staying at Woodhall Spa to take the waters, sent this card of the Eagle Lodge Hotel to her daughter, with the message: 'This is where I am staying. Isn't it a smart house.' The development of Woodhall Spa as a health hydro turned the little town into a resort.

▼ It is the late 1950s and passenger services have been withdrawn, but the branch is still busy with freight. A dirty and unkempt Ivatt Class 4 locomotive waits to take the local mixed freight out of Horncastle yard. This kind of activity was a regular sight until the closure of the line in 1971.

G.E.R. SP
From IPSWICH TO
HORNCASTLE
via G.N. & G.E. Joint Line and Spalding.

▲ The end of the line at Horncastle in the days of the LNER, with a typical branch line train waiting for custom under the little platform cover. A line of cattle wagons on the left hints at the kind of traffic that kept rural branches such as this in business.

43095

Central England: Woodhall to Horncastle

▼ At Woodhall Junction, the Horncastle branch and the former main line linking Lincoln and Boston live on, except for the track and the trains. The station buildings are now a private home, generously adorned with railway relics.

put the place on the map. By the 1940s all this was over, and the railway was in decline. Services were worked by old survivors from the days of the Great Northern, including a set of articulated carriages and various locomotives that had seen better days. British Railways carried on for a few years more and then withdrew passenger services in September 1954, despite strong local opposition. The branch remained open for freight until 1971.

▶ Seen here in winter sunshine and with a light covering of snow, the Spa Trail crosses the open Lincolnshire landscape, marking the route of the Horncastle branch. In other circumstances, a level railway with little significant engineering would probably have disappeared back into the landscape.

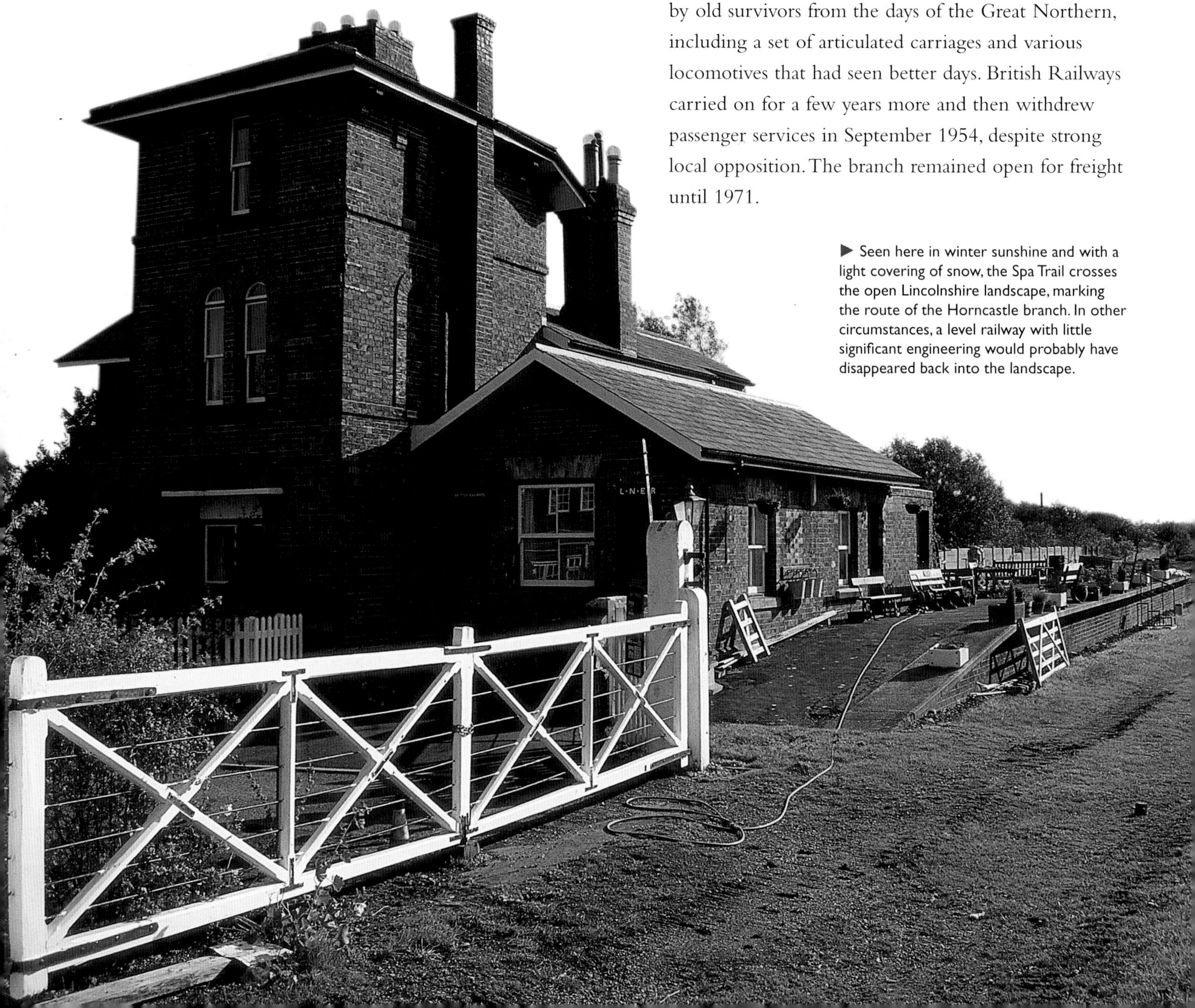

▲ An Edwardian view of Woodhall Spa station, with its rural main street. A cart piled with baggage is on its way to or from one of the smart hotels catering for the popular appeal of the spa's waters.

The Spa Trail

Since closure, the branch has been given a new lease of life as a path for walkers and cyclists, known as the Spa Trail, part of the Viking Way from Oakham to Barton-on-Humber. The trackbed crosses this flat, peaceful landscape, with little else to hint at the comings and goings of the railway in its heyday. Horncastle station is long gone, but Woodhall Junction survives, with other relics of the railway, as a private house.

Buxton to Ashbourne and High Peak Junction

Two rival railways arrived in Buxton in 1863, the LNWR and the Midland, both keen to exploit this famous spa town's appeal.

THE PAVILION, BUXTON

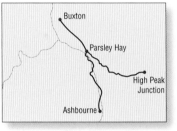

At the insistence of the Duke of Devonshire, who owned much of the town and wanted to ensure that modern developments were in keeping with Buxton's architectural traditions, two matching stations were built side by side, handsome stone-built train sheds with large semi-circular windows in the gable ends. This striking and, in railway terms, unique pair of buildings was destroyed, except for one gable end left standing in a pointless way, when it all closed in 1967.

Mineral lines and later additions complicated the railway map around Buxton, notably a route southwards to Ashbourne, opened by the LNWR in 1892. This met the existing branch to Ashbourne, built by the North Staffordshire Railway from Stoke and Uttoxeter in 1852, and enabled trains to run from Buxton through to Burton and beyond. The upper section of this LNWR route, from Hindlow, south of Buxton, to Parsley Hay, used the track of one of Britain's most remarkable railways, the Cromford & High Peak. Conceived originally as a canal to link the Cromford Canal to the Peak Forest Canal at Whaley Bridge, this was built as a railway from 1830, but canal engineering determined its nature. Over its 33 miles, it climbed 976 feet from Cromford and descended 745 feet to Whaley Bridge.

▲ A famous spa resort at least since the eighteenth century, Buxton enjoyed enormous popularity during the Victorian and Edwardian periods, thanks in part to the railway. Theatres and the Pavilion were added to the town's existing attractions and, at the time of this card, it was a very smart place indeed.

▶ An ancient tradition of many villages of the Derbyshire Peak district is the dressing of local wells with images and patterns made from flowers. Several of these villages are close to this line, for example Tissington.

[88]

▶ The Derbyshire scenery was perennially popular, and the railways that crossed it did all they could to encourage tourist traffic. This official LNWR card, issued before 1914, shows Raven's Tor in Bradford Dale, a spot accessible from Parsley Hay station, on the Buxton to Ashbourne route.

▼ Stone traffic was the justification for a number of lines built through the demanding Derbyshire landscape, and the importance of this continues today. In this 1961 photograph, a limestone train heads northwards towards Buxton, hauled by an elderly LMS goods locomotive.

RAVEN'S TOR, BRADFORD DALE
PARSLEY HAY STN L & N.W. RAILWAY

44339

◄ The Tissington Trail is one of the most popular of the cycleways created along former railway lines, as this photograph indicates. The 14-mile route is an exciting mixture of glorious scenery and railway history.

▼ The LNWR issued a great number of postcards before 1914 to promote tourist traffic on its Derbyshire routes, and many famous places were featured, whether they were on a railway or not. The Lion Rock, Dovedale, is to the west of Ashbourne.

THE LION ROCK DOVEDALE

The route was winding, following contour lines, there were three tunnels, long lengths of stone-faced embankments and, where there would have been flights of locks, there were nine inclined planes, up which wagons were dragged on chains or ropes powered by stationary steam engines. Wagons were initially pulled by horses on the level sections, but steam locomotives were introduced from 1833. Primary traffic was limestone but there were limited passenger facilities until 1876. From the 1860s, when the LNWR took over, the route was straightened and simplified, and the number of inclines reduced to seven. However, the process of travel remained slow and complex along a railway that was essentially a pre-Victorian concept. What is even more remarkable is that a large part of the route remained in use until the mid-1960s, when this veritable antique was finally abandoned, with the lines to Ashbourne. Buxton still has a station, but the connecting line south to Matlock and Cromford went at the same time. Peak Rail plan to re-open it as a preserved line. South of Buxton, small parts of the network survive, serving the local quarries.

▼ Parts of the Cromford & High Peak line, by then an extraordinary anachronism, were still in use in 1966. Here, an Austerity tank rounds Gotham Curve. The stone-faced embankment is typical of the line.

THE MARKET PLACE, ASHBOURNE

◀ Ashbourne received its first railway in 1854, and the line from Buxton arrived 40 years later. From that point onwards, this traditional Derbyshire market town became a popular resort and a useful base for visits to the Peak District. This card shows the market place in about 1910.

▶ The unique features of the Cromford & High Peak Railway drew many visitors while it was still in operation. Here, a group from a visiting rail tour pose at the top of Sheep Pasture Incline in September 1953.

The route today

Today the major parts of the route, from High Peak Junction near Cromford north to Downlow (the High Peak Trail) and from Parsley Hay south to Ashbourne (the Tissington Trail), form a long-distance cycle track, one of the best in Britain. In total it offers over 30 miles of cycling through glorious Derbyshire scenery, along well-surfaced tracks, and with countless opportunities to admire the extraordinary achievements of the early nineteenth-century railway builders, to whom every obstacle was merely a challenge to be overcome. Inclines, tunnels, bridges and embankments survive, along with an engine house, goods sheds, warehouses and other relics. For those not excited by railway trails, there are classic Derbyshire villages, Hartington and Tissington, and the eternal pleasures of the landscape.

▼ In its last years the Cromford & High Peak was much visited by photographers keen to capture its unique qualities. This was taken in 1966 by Ivo Peters, a well-known railway photographer. The locomotive's crew look as if they have already posed a number of times.

Cheltenham to King's Sutton

The railway from Cheltenham to King's Sutton was a meandering route, mostly through the attractive landscape of the Cotswolds. It was always a typical rural railway and by the late 1940s there was only one through train a day, which took three hours to cover the 44 miles, allowing plenty of time to enjoy the scenery.

A s with so many minor lines, the history was complicated. It started in the 1850s with the Chipping Norton Railway, a short line connecting the town with the main Oxford-to-Worcester line at Kingham (then known as Chipping Norton Junction). By 1862 passenger services had ceased. Next came the Bourton-on-the-Water Railway, whose short line westwards from Kingham opened in 1862. Plans to carry on to Cheltenham got nowhere.

▲ Unexpected things can still be seen on long-lost railways, such as this battered but still identifiable concrete gradient post, east of Stow-on-the-Wold.

▼ This view of Notgrove was taken shortly before the line's closure in 1962. The train drifts into a deserted station on a summer's day, and the photographer's shadow is the only sign of life on the platform. There is not much to see today, as nature has reclaimed the site.

▲ Kingham, known as Chipping Norton Junction until 1909, was a busy place. The lines towards King's Sutton branch away on the right; in the distance, over the passenger's head, is the bridge carrying the Cheltenham line. Today, the station is still open on the Oxford-to-Worcester line, but the bridge, signal box and all other structures are gone.

▶ Rollright Halt was one of a number of minor stations along the line. This early picture shows the typical GWR pagoda-style shelter used in such locations. Today the embankment is overgrown and inaccessible and the bridge over the lane has gone, but the house is still there.

◄ The most accessible part of the route today is the area around Hook Norton tunnel, which is a nature reserve and footpath. The tunnel itself is bricked up but this bridge survives to the north of it.

▼ In landscape terms, the Hook Norton area is the most dramatic. The steep hills and valleys demanded deep cuttings, a tunnel and a high viaduct, whose tall stone piers still dominate the valley. This picture of Hook Norton station, with its steep approach, indicates the nature of the landscape. It is a complete railway scene, but nothing remains today.

▼ (*Inset*) Bloxham station has gone and much of its site is now covered in houses. A metal footbridge survives, crossing the overgrown bit that remains, but seems to lead nowhere.

Nothing then happened until the 1880s, when another company, the Banbury & Cheltenham Direct, completed the missing sections from Bourton to Cheltenham and from Chipping Norton to King's Sutton on the Oxford-to-Banbury line. By 1897 it was absorbed into the GWR. The landscape made its own demands, with plenty of cuttings and embankments, a tunnel and a dramatic viaduct near Hook Norton. Never busy, the line was destined to close at some point and this process started in 1951, with the Chipping Norton to King's Sutton section. The rest followed eleven years later.

Today, the remains of the line reflect the different closure periods. West of Kingham, many of the distinctive engineering-brick bridges survive, while on the eastern section most of the bridges have gone. Starting from Cheltenham, there is not much to be seen before Andoversford but eastwards from here the line can be traced through the hills and valleys in cuttings and embankments, clearly visible but largely inaccessible. Near Bourton the line follows the valley of the Windrush, and in Bourton the station unexpectedly survives, locked in a council yard. Kingham, now a simple station with an old GWR nameboard, was much more significant and the site of the former junction can be explored on footpaths. An industrial park has taken over much of the route around Chipping Norton but to the east the sites of remote halts can be traced. The approach to Hook Norton is now a nature reserve, with footpath access. In Bloxham the station site is largely built over but, incongruously, a footbridge survives, though inaccessible. Adderbury station is also an industrial site, even though this section remained open for goods for a few years. At King's Sutton modern trains roar through, but the old bay platform can still be identified, along with the site of the old junction.

◄ King's Sutton station is, remarkably, still alive, though most trains, like this Birmingham-bound Virgin Voyager, just race through. The remains of another platform can be seen on the left, while in the distance beyond the bridge a line of trees on the right marks the site of the junction with the Cheltenham line.

Cheltenham to Andover

By the 1880s the railway map of Britain was quite comprehensive. Most main lines were in place and the network's tentacles had spread into many corners of the country. However, railway building never ceased, despite the economic unpredictabiliy of the late Victorian era.

The 1880s saw the construction of many branch and local connecting lines, to encourage freight traffic, feeder services to main lines and holiday business to the expanding coastal and inland resorts. Few new railways made great profits, but there always seemed to be plenty of investors and speculators prepared to put their money into railway projects, particularly when such projects seemed to fill a gap on the map. Several fairly substantial new railways were planned at this time, cross-country lines that seemed to offer more direct routes between major centres of conurbation and industry than already existed. A primary example was the line from Cheltenham to Andover, a long, rural north-to-south route whose strengths appeared to be its connection – Cheltenham, Andoversford, Swindon, Grafton and Andover – with

▲ Cheltenham's classic elegance has long been popular, as this Edwardian card indicates. The first railway arrived in 1840, with a grand, country house-like station called Lansdown. Other stations followed – Malvern Road and St James, for the GWR, and High Street, opened by the Midland in 1862.

▶ A quiet life and limited traffic made the M&SWJR an old-fashioned operation, even in the days of British Railways. This museum-like photograph shows the interior of the signal box at Andoversford Junction in 1961, when it was very near the end of its life. This is the box shown in the photograph opposite.

important east–west routes, and thus its possibilities as a connecting line between the south and the Midlands. It was built from the early 1880s by two separate companies, the Swindon & Cheltenham Extension Railway and the Swindon, Marlborough & Andover Railway. Construction took some time and the line was not completed until 1891, by which time the two companies had merged to form themselves into the grandly named Midland & South Western Junction Railway. The aim was to run trains beyond Andover to Southampton via existing lines, but this was not achieved until 1894. The great hopes that had inspired the railway were never fulfilled, partly because the route itself was too rural and remote to generate much internal traffic and partly because the anticipated heavy through traffic from Southampton and the South to the Midlands never materialized. The railway went bankrupt in the 1890s, recovered and then managed to operate successfully until

▼ On a warm autumn afternoon in 1955 the Cheltenham to Southampton train arrives at Andoversford Junction, hauled by an old GWR Mogul, ready for the long cross-country route south.

London and South Western Ry. 787
From WATERLOO TO
Dowdeswell
Via Andover Junction.

▲ This classic lost railway scene is Withington station, to the south of Andoversford, in 2005. Platforms and overbridge still stand as relics of the railway age, but they are now as mysterious as the structures of long-forgotten civilizations in the jungles of South America. It is hard to believe that trains stopped here less than fifty years ago. The real legacy of the closure programme of the 1960s is secret places like this, all over Britain.

1923, when it was absorbed into the GWR. Its salvation was military traffic, as the southern section served several bases, depots, camps and training areas, and the line was heavily used during both World Wars. By the late 1950s there was little traffic, and the route was a natural candidate for closure. It disappeared in 1961, along with many of its connecting lines. In the process Cirencester and Marlborough lost their mainline railway links. All that survived was the section

north of Andover to the military stores depot at Ludgershall, and this is still used.

The route today

Although it took a long time to build, the Midland & South Western Junction was not a heavily engineered line. Its route is primarily through an open landscape of farmland and rolling hills, crossed by river valleys, notably the head waters of the Coln, Kennet and Thames. Today the open landscape makes it possible to trace much of the route, although it is not always accessible. Andoversford, the site of the junction with lines to Banbury and Oxford, is worth exploring. Part of Cirencester's old Town station survives, but this was on the other line, the branch from Kemble, opened in the 1840s. To the south, the remains of a viaduct can be seen near South Cerney. Near Blunsdon, between Cricklade and Swindon, a short section has been re-opened as a preserved line by the Swindon & Cricklade Railway. From the outskirts of Swindon cyclists and walkers can follow the old trackbed through the village of Chiseldon and then through open countryside all the way to Marlborough. A bridlepath runs parallel for much of the way.

▼ Cirencester's M&SWJR station was Watermoor, away from the town centre. In 1961 it was in its death throes, with closure imminent. On a summer evening, the Swindon Town train, now just a couple of carriages in the care of an old GWR tank locomotive, pauses at Watermoor. The company's workshops were at Cirencester.

▲ In a typical landscape of woods and gentle hills, an Andover to Cheltenham train crosses a small bridge near Withington, south of Andoversford, in the summer of 1961. The setting, the unhurried atmosphere and the elderly Southern Railway locomotive all capture the flavour of the country railway in its dying years. Within a few months the line had closed and all this had been consigned to history.

CIRENCESTER
WATERMOOR

► The M&SWJR built Swindon Town station to the south of the huge GWR workshop complex and its busy London to Bristol route. This photograph was taken in the early twentieth century, when the line was still reasonably busy.

▼ In a complicated coming together of lines at Wolfhall and Grafton Junctions, the M&SWJR met and crossed the GWR's main line west from Reading and its branch to Marlborough. In 1957, in a landscape setting typical of the route as a whole, a southbound train pauses at Wolfhall Junction.

▶ While it never had particular tourist appeal, Andover did its best in the Edwardian period to put itself on the map. According to this card posted in 1911, the station was one of the town's highlights. There were actually two stations, the main Junction one, on the LSWR's main line west and the terminus of the M&SWJR's line, and Town station, which despite its name was well to the south on a connecting line to Stockbridge and Romsey along the Test valley.

▼ Railway life has returned to a small part of the route, in the form of the Swindon & Cricklade Railway, a GWR-style preserved line. This is Blunsdon station, the railway's headquarters and depot.

There is plenty to be seen between Marlborough and Grafton Junction as the route runs west of Savernake Forest and close to the Kennet & Avon Canal, but the story is complicated here. A branch to Marlborough was opened in 1864 and was initially incorporated into the M&SWJR's route. Traffic congestion resulted, so in 1896 the M&SWJ built a bypass called the Marlborough & Grafton Railway. Both then remained in service until 1933, when the original line was closed. South of Grafton the railway ran through an open landscape of gentle, bare hills, and nearly all the route to Andover survives, on low embankments or cut into the slopes of the hillside. Few structures remain, apart from small accommodation bridges. This has long been, and still is, military territory, with the army supplying plenty of traffic during the first half of the twentieth century. A branch served the base at Tidworth, and the line between Ludgershall and Andover is still open for army use.

Whitland to Cardigan

There were a number of schemes from the 1850s onwards to build railways to Cardigan. The Carmarthen & Cardigan Railway, incorporated in 1854, planned to link the two towns, but in the event only part of its route was built.

PICTURESQUE CARDIGANSHIRE
KILGERRAN CASTLE

Cardigan remained isolated from the railway network until 1886, when the Whitland & Cardigan Railway was opened. This was itself an extension of an existing line, built by the Whitland & Taf Vale Railway to Crymmych Arms twelve years earlier. Never really independent, Cardigan's railway was operated from the

▼ On 8 September 1962, a couple of days before the closure of the line, a two-coach train pauses at Glogue halt while the locomotive takes on water. It is a busy scene, with many coming to see the train for the last time. Even a dog has stopped to watch. Today the grass-covered platform survives, along with parts of the crossing gates, now smartly painted.

start by the GWR, which took control from 1890. At that time, this old market town, with a long history as a vital crossing point on the Teifi, was beginning to attract tourists, many of whom were drawn to the site of the castle, where the first national eisteddfod was held by Rhys ap Gruffyd, then the ruler of south Wales. The castle itself, built by Richard I, was destroyed during the Civil War. Cardigan was also

◄ This Edwardian card of Kilgerran Castle highlights one of the major architectural features of the route. Wonderfully sited above the Teifi, this Norman castle, rebuilt by Edward III, was a royal residence in the fifteenth century.

▼ On a leisurely afternoon in 1961, a train for Whitland waits in Cardigan station. There is plenty of time for chatting while the guard's van is loaded. By this time, few passengers were using the line, and the journey was too slow to attract a new generation of tourists already committed to the freedom offered by the car.

◄ East of Cardigan the trackbed is now an official path. For a while it follows the tidal Teifi, a popular route to a nature reserve on marsh and estuary land south of the river.

◀ This old postcard, probably based on a photograph from the 1930s, shows Cardigan's High Street, with plenty of period detail. A busy harbour established Cardigan's wealth, but it had silted up long before the coming of the railway. By then, farming, fishing and tourism were the mainstay of the town, and its railway.

▼ At the end of its life, the railway slips quietly towards oblivion. On the last day of passenger services, a train for Whitland waits in Cardigan's single platform, the usual two carriages hauled by one of GWR's ubiquitous tank locomotives. Only a few people have turned out to watch the ending of an era. A well-dressed family group in the distance, probably seeing off visiting relatives, is using the railway as it had always been used, as the mainstay of community life.

HIGH STREET, CARDIGAN.

once a busy port, but this trade had been lost because of the silting up of the river estuary. Fishing was still important, and visitors were beginning to explore the coastline and beaches near by. The railway was therefore seen by the town as a lifeline, and a new source of revenue. In the event, it was never really busy but it remained the town's main link with the outside world until the 1920s.

The railway was an essentially local enterprise. The 27-mile journey took over an hour and a half, with nine intermediate stops between Whitland and Cardigan. Several were halts serving small, isolated communities. Having reached Whitland, travellers were still a long way from Carmarthen, the nearest town of any size. Up to the 1930s the pace of life in rural west Wales made this unimportant, but the spread of road transport in the 1950s changed that, and by the early 1960s there were only three or four trains each way on weekdays, carrying few passengers. The line was an early candidate for closure, which took place on 10 September 1962, shortly before the publication of Dr Beeching's report. Freight lingered on a few more months.

Despite its unremarkable life, the Cardigan branch offered passengers a delightful journey, as the train wound its way along wooded valleys, following the meanderings of little streams that made their way northwards towards the grander valley of the Teifi. It was a journey that showed the landscape of west Wales at its best. Had it survived, it would be a popular tourist railway.

◀ Near Login, a former halt two stops up the line from Whitland, gates still mark the site of the level crossing. On a bright morning in early spring, it is easy to imagine the local train trundling out of the woods and whistling as it approaches the crossing. In scenes such as this, the Cardigan branch survives in the landscape.

Looking for clues

Tracing the railway brings to life some of that journey, even though much of the route is remote and inaccessible. Like the journey itself, it is a slow process, for only minor roads follow the line, and in a random way. However, the sites of most of the various stations and halts can be found. In Cardigan itself nothing remains of the railway, and the site of the junction near Whitland is impenetrable. But in other places, railway buildings and structures can be identified. At Llanglydwen, for example, the station buildings still overlook the old coal yard, a reminder of the importance of the coal

trade even to a minor railway. And at Glogue, where the platform survives, the scant remains of the crossing gates are carefully preserved and freshly painted. Elsewhere, the railway's leisurely route through the landscape is indicated by surviving embankments and the remains of bridges. The line's final approach to Cardigan, following the curve of the tidal Teifi through what is now a nature reserve, is a footpath. This short section shows how the whole route would make an excellent footpath and cycleway, but sadly much of it is privately owned and so detailed exploration is not possible.

Gaerwen to Amlwch

One of Britain's best-known railways is the line to Holyhead, engineered by George Stephenson and opened throughout in 1850. The most significant part was that built by the Chester & Holyhead Railway, incorporating as it did grand and revolutionary viaducts at Conwy and across the Menai Straits.

SEA BATHS, BULL BAY, AMLWCH

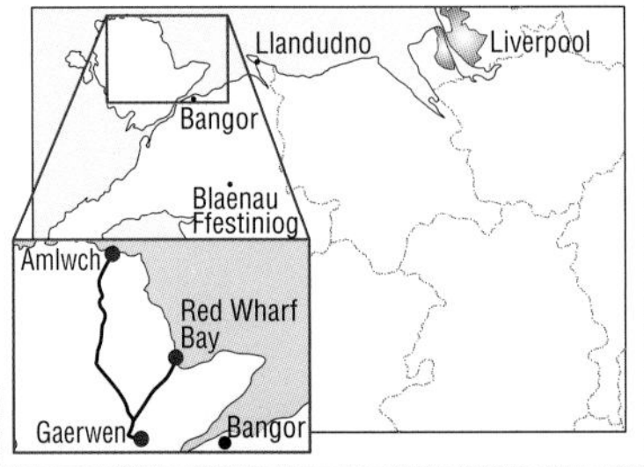

▼ Amlwch was a pretty station with some decorative cast-iron details, platform flower beds, and a station name board with letters made from rope. This scene shows a few passengers about to board the diesel railcar for Bangor. Here, as elsewhere in Britain, these vehicles were introduced in the early 1960s to try to keep the branch alive – but to little avail.

BANGOR

◀ Issued by the L&NWR before World War I, and overprinted on the reverse by that company for use as a receipt for correspondence, this card of Bull Bay and the castle was part of an official series promoting tourism in north Wales, with the general heading: 'Visit North Wales for a charming holiday.'

▲ A wet day at the simple wooden terminus station at Red Wharf Bay, probably in the late 1940s. Passenger traffic had gone in 1930, but freight lingered on until 1950. By now run down and untidy, the station building, still in LMS colours, is dominated by the Portland Cement advert.

In 1859 this became part of the L&NWR, the forerunner of the LMS. Eight years later, an independent company, the Anglesey Central Railway, opened a branch from Gaerwen on the main line to Amlwch. This was followed by another branch, to Red Wharf Bay. In 1876 these were bought by the L&NWR for £80,000, and in 1923 they all passed into the care of the LMS. The branches were generally served by trains from Bangor, on the mainland.

Lack of traffic, and particularly the shortage of hoped-for tourists, made the Red Wharf Bay branch an early closure victim. Passenger services were withdrawn in 1930, and freight in 1950. Amlwch, however, was a different story. Its busy harbour, combined with some local industry, its fine beaches and the sea baths at Bull Bay, gave lasting appeal to a town first developed by the Romans to take advantage of the nearby copper deposits. As a result, train services were maintained well into the British Railways era, and the end of passenger services did not come until December 1964. Even at that point, the line did not die completely, as it remained open for many years to carry traffic from a chemical works near Amlwch.

Closed, but not lost

Despite being closed for over fifty years, the short branch to Red Wharf Bay can still be traced in the landscape. Remote, rural and generally inaccessible, the route can be followed from minor roads. Bridges are in place, but the trackbed is often an impenetrable jungle. The most visible section is on the approach to Red Wharf Bay, where an embankment crosses fields either side of a former level crossing.

◀ As the Amlwch branch approaches the junction at Gaerwen, all seems nearly normal. The track and the points are there, and the signal waits. Only the encroaching gorse shows there have been no trains for years.

▼ In the late 1950s the line was still steam operated. The train is ready to leave, the guard checks his watch, but the place is deserted.

◄ In the last fifty years much of the line to Red Wharf Bay has disappeared, but in some places there are still visible traces. This section of embankment, now the province of sheep, crosses the surrounding farmland on the approach to Red Wharf Bay.

▼ Amlwch has an ancient tidal harbour which, by the time this card was printed in the 1930s, was as much picturesque as practical. Here, at low tide, it is filled with three coastal trading vessels and a couple of small steamers. The photograph is probably older than the postcard.

The line to Amlwch is much more unusual. The branch has been closed for some years, following the end of the chemical factory traffic but, unexpectedly, everything is still in place, track and sleepers, crossing gates, signs and signals. In some places, it looks as though the trains could still run, while in others the track has been buried beneath encroaching greenery, gorse, shrubs and a variety of flowers, including bluebells and valerian. The stations have mostly become private houses, but the line still runs past the old platforms. One, at Pentre Berw, has been restored and is now decorated with old signs. Even the old military branch north of Rhosgoch still has its tracks. As a result, the branch line has an almost eerie presence all the way from the chemical works north of Amlwch, through the town with several level crossings, and then winding its way across the landscape to the junction at Gaerwen, where a signal stands as though waiting to let trains out on to the main line, busy with traffic to and from Holyhead. Much of the route is inaccessible and private, but following it is easy, from minor roads, tracks and footpaths. It is a rare treat to explore a closed branch with a sense of railway reality. One day the trains may even return.

▲ Despite years of closure, the Amlwch branch has all its track and infrastructure. Even the notices are still in place. Near Gaerwen the single line begins, but trains would have a hard time forcing their way though the plantlife that has taken over.

Ruabon to Barmouth and Blaenau Ffestiniog

The railway from Ruabon to Barmouth was the creation of the GWR, ambitious to extend its empire to the west coast of Wales.

B. 39398. LLANGOLLEN: FROM THE BRIDGE.

▲ The most important structure on the Bala to Blaenau line is Cwm Prysor viaduct, seen here from an approaching train in 1959. Today this still stands, a monument to a little-used line that struggled through a tough and often spectacular landscape to no great benefit for its builders and investors in the 1870s.

◀ (Inset) Posted in 1912, this card shows the River Dee and the adjacent station in Llangollen. By this time the tourist traffic was becoming significant and the station was often busy. Today, as the terminus of the Llangollen Railway, the station looks remarkably similar, although its style is the GWR of later years. Until the line was closed in the 1960s, trains continued off the bottom of the postcard to Ruabon, or away into the trees towards Barmouth.

◀ A landscape of gentle hills, woods and small fields accompanies the line on its route along the Dee valley west of Llangollen. In the 1960s, with closure on the horizon, a local train makes its way along the valley near Glyndyfrydwy, hauled by a GWR tank engine.

It was built in short stages by nominally independent companies. The Vale of Llangollen Railway opened in 1862 and the Llangollen & Corwen's nine-mile line opened four years later. In 1868 the Corwen & Bala opened its short section, and the route was finally completed in 1870 by the Bala & Dolgelly Railway, which made an end-on connection with a short branch from Barmouth along the Mawddach estuary. To the south an equally tortuous scheme linked Welshpool with Machynlleth and the Cambrian Coast route, built by several companies that came together in 1864 to form Cambrian Railways, to the annoyance of the GWR. In time, the rivalry between the Cambrian and the GWR became intense, and at Dolgellau, where their routes met, they built separate stations. To some extent these two routes duplicated each other and both served a region that had neither a great population nor much in the way of industry and mineral resources. However, that was not the point. The main function of these lines was to give a degree of control in central west Wales to the GWR, whose primary aim was keeping the LNWR at bay. In the end, they all became part of the GWR.

In time, the Ruabon to Barmouth line became a heavily used freight route,

▲ The Bala & Dolgelly Railway, completed in 1870, was part of a route that crossed Wales from Barmouth to Ruabon, with important connections along the way. The line was closed in 1965. This shows the once-pretty station at Dolgellau, at the western end, some years later.

▼ Set against a dramatic sunset, a train bound for Ruabon crosses Barmouth viaduct in February 1965 on the first stage of its journey through the centre of Wales. The train has just left the three steel arches on the Barmouth end, the centre one of which could be swung to allow the passage of ships. The rest of the viaduct is wooden.

offering an alternative link from south Wales to the Midlands and the north via Carmarthen, Aberystwyth, Wrexham and Chester along GWR tracks. It was also kept busy with local cargoes, agricultural produce, livestock, timber and minerals.

The Beeching plan required only one route to the west coast of Wales and that was the Machynlleth line. All others were closed in the 1960s. Since then, parts of the Ruabon to Barmouth route have been re-opened as steam tourist lines. The Llangollen Railway operates standard-gauge services westwards towards Corwen, along the valley of the Dee, while further to the west the narrow-gauge Bala Lake Railway runs for a shorter distance along the southern shore of Lake Bala to Llanuwchllyn. As a result, little of the route is totally lost and exploration is easy, though more limited at the Ruabon end. At the other end, the section from Dolgellau to Barmouth is a cycle track, which is the perfect way to experience the delights of the Mawddach estuary. Most remote and harder to explore is the central section, from Corwen westwards to Bala, though the trackbed is often accessible from nearby roads.

◀ Seen here in the 1960s, Bala Lake Halt, also known as Bala Penybont, was a little-used station on the Barmouth line. Even the campers in the field have come by car. Today, this spot is alive again, as the Bala Lake Railway.

Bala to Blaenau Ffestiniog

The GWR's ambitions were not limited to west Wales and the coast, for they also had their eyes on the north Wales slate traffic, and Blaenau Ffestiniog in particular. Unfortunately, the LNWR had similar ideas and began to plan an attack from the north, via an extension of the existing Conwy valley line. The GWR responded by backing the Bala & Festiniog Railway, whose 22-mile route from the south across difficult and hilly terrain was given approval in 1873. The race was on but, as both lines

proved laborious and expensive to construct, it went rather slowly. In the event, the LNWR won, and its trains reached Blaenau in 1881. The GWR finally limped past the finishing post two years later. Both were able to benefit from the slate trade, but the legacy of their competition was that Blaenau Ffestiniog had two mainline stations, a couple of hundred yards apart but with no railway connection. This bizarre situation remained until 1960, when the GWR route south to Bala was closed in connection with the building of a nuclear power station at Llyn Trawsfynydd. As this was to be serviced via the Conwy valley line, a connection had to be made in 1961. Later, Blaenau gained a new terminus station, built on the site of the old GWR one, and now used jointly by Conwy valley trains and the Ffestiniog Railway's narrow-gauge line from Porthmadog.

Exploration of the old GWR line to Blaenau is exciting as plenty survives in the wild landscape. There is not much to be seen in Bala itself but north of the town the route is

◀ Photographed at the time of closure, Bala station already has an abandoned air. This is the town station, at the beginning of the branch to Blaenau. The junction station, though fully equipped, was rarely used by Bala passengers, and a shuttle train ran between the two for those using mainline trains at the junction.

▼ The most dramatic section of the line is around Cwm Prysor, where the trackbed can still be traced as it follows the contours and curves of the hillside. In this misty view taken in the 1990s from the trackbed in the foreground, the line of the old railway can be seen curving to the right above the steep fields. It is then carved into the rocky hillside in the distance.

▼ Long trains unload soldiers and their equipment at Trawsfynydd before World War I, perhaps Territorials at their annual camp in the area. Both tracks are being used, and one train includes a group of horse boxes. At this point the station is still being built; the platforms are unsurfaced, the lavatories await their roof, and the lamp standards their lamps.

TRAWSFYNYDD NEW STATION.

clear. At Frongoch the station survives as a private house, then the trackbed climbs into wilder country before vanishing into the waters of Llyn Celyn reservoir, whose construction closed the line in 1960. The best section is around Cwm Prysor, with the trackbed alternating between embankments and cuttings. Often set on a ledge cut into the sweeping contours of the rocky hillside, it is seen easily from minor roads far below. It must have been a spectacular line, with echoes of railways in the Alps or South America. Surviving bridges and embankments hint at something far more ancient and intriguing than a minor Victorian branch line. The line drops down the Prysor valley to Trawsfynydd, to a landscape of softer hills, woods and farms. The railway was kept open to this point, to serve the power station during its lifetime, so the route onwards to Blaenau is easy to follow.

◀ In the spring of 1959 a Bala-bound train waits to depart from the former GWR terminus station, proudly called Blaenau Ffestiniog Central. The single carriage and the deserted air suggests that passengers were already rare. The other Blaenau station, for the Conwy valley line, is in the distance, overshadowed by the towering slate hills that determine the town's character.

▼ With the driver keeping an eye on the track ahead, the train from Bala approaches Blaenau in 1959, along a stretch of track set on a curving embankment to the south of the town. The character of Blaenau is apparent, surrounded by slate hills, and with terraces of houses roofed in the characteristic colour of the local slate. Until recently, this part of the route was still used for power-station traffic.

Carmarthen to Aberystwyth

Two of the most important stations in west Wales in the heyday of the railway were Aberystwyth and Carmarthen. Today they are shadows of their former selves.

▲ This busy scene of horses being unloaded on to a crowded platform for Lampeter Fair in about 1912 shows how vital the railway was in the life of small rural communities.

▼ As a major rail centre, Carmarthen had a large and well-equipped station capable of handling mainline expresses, local services and a wide range of goods traffic, as shown by this 1930s view. Today the station, much reduced, is the end of the line, with buffers replacing the level crossing.

Aberystwyth was the end of a meandering branch from Dovey Junction; Carmarthen a terminus by default and an inconvenient reversal point for trains to Pembroke and Fishguard. It is still possible to travel by train between the two places but it would require an interminable and completely impractical journey via Shrewsbury, Craven Arms and Llanelli. Until the 1960s things were different, and it was possible to travel directly from Carmarthen to Aberystwyth, a 56-mile journey scheduled to take about 2 hours 30 minutes.

The story of this line goes back to 1854, and the setting up of the Carmarthen & Cardigan Railway. Constant financial problems limited progress and by 1864 it had only reached Pencader. Cardigan remained firmly out of reach. Eventually it was sorted out, largely by the GWR. The remains of the planned main line north of Pencader became the Newcastle Emlyn branch, opened in 1895, and a new main line was built up to Aberystwyth via Lampeter. Later came a branch to Aberaeron, opened by the Lampeter,

[124]

▼ Pencader, seen here in the 1950s still looking like a typical GWR country town station, was the junction for the Newcastle Emlyn branch. The nature of traffic on the line is shown by the oil tank wagon attached to the end of the passenger train.

Aberayron & New Quay Light Railway in 1911. Meanwhile, Cardigan did finally receive its own railway in 1886, but from a totally different direction, from Whitland, well to the west of Carmarthen. These railways served a predominantly rural and underpopulated region, with little industrial development, though freight traffic helped to keep them alive until the 1950s. From the Edwardian era, the rise of tourism also helped, particularly for Aberystwyth and the branches to the coast. However, closures were eventually inevitable. First to go was the Aberaeron branch in 1951, followed by Newcastle Emlyn a year later. The main line disappeared in 1965.

Since then, two sections have become preserved lines, the Gwili Railway based on Bronwydd Arms, north of Carmarthen, and the narrow-gauge Teifi Valley Railway around Henllan, on the former Newcastle Emlyn branch. For much of its route, the railway followed river valleys, the Gwili, the Teifi and the Ystwyth, and can still be traced today, though some sections are inaccessible or private. There is nothing to be seen north of Carmarthen until the start of the Gwili Railway. Pencader station has gone, but Llanybydder survives. Near Lampeter the bridge over the Teifi is still there. North of Lampeter the railway crossed a more open landscape, and its route can be followed from parallel roads. From higher ground it is clearly seen following the river valleys, notably near Ystrad Meurig Castle. Near Llanilar part of the route is a footpath and cycleway. At Aberystwyth the grand former GWR station is still in use.

Wales: Carmarthen to Aberystwyth

◄ Llanrhystyd Road was the first station on the line south from Aberystwyth. In the 1950s, when this photograph was taken, there were only four trains a day each way to keep the stationmaster occupied.

▼ Aberystwyth station was built by the Cambrian Railway in 1864, but much of what can be seen today reflects later work by the GWR, mostly in the 1920s.

◄ Much of the route of the line can be traced, and there are a number of tangible reminders of its life, including this metal bridge across the Teifi near Lampeter.

▼ West of Llanilar, the route can be seen as a low embankment along the valley, marked by a line of trees. This is a familiar way of identifying a lost railway in the landscape.

The Wharfe below Grassington Bridge.

Northern England

Alne to Easingwold

A dangerous mixture of enthusiasm and optimism inspired the building of many minor railways in late Victorian Britain. It was a time when every town of any stature had to be part of the ever-expanding railway network.

Easingwold was just such a place, a small market town with a population of about 2,000 and some ambitious local businessmen who believed that trade could not develop properly without a railway. They set to work, raising support and money for the building of a branch line to connect Easingwold with the busy main line of the North Eastern Railway less than 3 miles away at Alne, another small market town, to the north of York. Authorized in August 1887, the Easingwold Railway was completed in July 1891, with construction costs of £17,000.

▲ Most of the Easingwold Railway has vanished back into the fields, but unexpected traces can still be found. This old 1950s van body is quietly decaying by a farmyard not far from Easingwold. The doors indicate that this was an early type of container, transported on flat wagons. The route of the line was by the distant line of trees, across the field on the left.

▲ Towards the end of its life, the branch to Easingwold, by then threatened with closure, was popular with railtours. At Alne, in the summer of 1957, passengers on the Yorkshire Coast Railtour scramble to mount the open wagons in which they will travel. Such scenes of simple enthusiasm, once commonplace, are inconceivable in the Health & Safety age.

◀ It is the summer of 1952, and Easingwold Railway maintains its independence into the era of British Railways. By then passenger carrying had ceased, but at least one of the line's antiquated carriages was still in use, seen here shunted against the buffers. In the background, cattle wagons show that the line was still busy with agricultural traffic.

The Easingwold Railway was from the start fiercely independent. It owned its own locomotives, two small tank engines, which continued to haul trains up and down the short line for much of its life. When these were in need of repair, replacements were hired from the NER. Carriages, mostly old four- or six-wheel vehicles, were acquired as cast-offs from larger companies. In the end, the NER operated the line, but the company remained independent. It survived the grouping of 1923, never becoming part of the LNER, and in 1928 underlined its independence by renaming itself the Easingwold Light Railway. More remarkably, it escaped the all-encompassing net of British Railways when the network was nationalized in January 1948. Perhaps it was

◄ The best memorial to the branch is the Old Station House, formerly the station hotel at Easingwold. Though now surrounded by modern housing, this grand building reflects the pride with which the line was constructed.

▼ The track and platform are overgrown, but a few trains still run. In this 1957 photograph, staff and onlookers wander away, while three people stand waving at the departing train. As passenger carrying had long since ceased, they are probably saying farewell to a visiting railtour group. The photographer must have been standing on the guard's van. The house on the right was once the station hotel.

► A typical Easingwold train, an ancient carriage and one of the railway's two tank locomotives, waits in the bay platform at Alne, beyond the tracks of the East Coast main line. Both vehicles carry the Easingwold's name and livery. On this warm day the driver and a lady friend pose for the camera.

too small and insignificant to attract the attention of the Whitehall bureaucrats. By then passenger traffic had dwindled to almost nothing, and in November 1948 the passenger service ceased. Freight, however, kept the line alive for another decade, with British Railways locomotives hauling the wagons to and fro. On 27 December 1957 the last train ran along the overgrown tracks of the Easingwold Railway.

Lost, but not forgotten

Over half a century after its closure, the lightly engineered Easingwold Railway might have been expected to have disappeared into history. Surprisingly, this is not the case.

There is no station today at Alne, and trains on the East Coast main line thunder through the huddle of buildings that indicate where

the station, and the junction, were once sited. From there the route across the flat Yorkshire landscape is initially hard to trace, and much of the trackbed has been ploughed out. On the approach to Easingwold, however, it is well defined, raised above the surrounding fields and partly hidden by bushes. New housing has now spread over the once extensive station site at Easingwold, but in the middle of this development, part of which is called Station Court, is the old station house, which was once the station hotel, a richly decorative and strongly built stone structure dated 1892, as well as a range of former offices and station buildings. These grand structures, reflective of the local ambition and pride that brought the railway into existence, are a fine memorial to a line that was famous for its independence.

Skipton to Grassington

The railways came early to Yorkshire, long before the dales were popular with visitors. Minerals and freight were the primary inspiration, as was the ambition shared by several companies to build the best route between the industrial towns of Lancashire and the north-east.

The Wharfe below Grassington Bridge.

The origins of the Grassington branch lay in just such a scheme, planned by the Liverpool, Manchester & Newcastle Junction Railway in 1846. This, and other schemes in the 1860s and 1880s, came to nothing, and it was the end of the century before the Yorkshire Dales were invaded by railways.

In 1895 the Yorkshire Dales Railway was formed to build a line from Embsay, near Skipton, to Darlington. In 1902 it was opened as far as Grassington. It never went any farther, for by that time these expensive cross-country routes no longer made economic sense. While the Yorkshire Dales Railway remained independent until 1923, the branch was always operated by the Midland Railway. Branch line services were augmented by through coaches to and from Bradford, making possible onward travel to London and other major cities. However, the line was never busy and regular passenger services were withdrawn in 1930. Ironically, this was just before the great rise in the popularity of walking in general and in the Yorkshire Dales in particular, and so the branch continued to be used by excursion trains.

▲ (Top) Grassington has long been one of the most popular of the Wharfedale villages, as reflected by this Edwardian view of the famous seventeenth-century bridge. Lead mining established the town's wealth, but tourism took over in the late Victorian period, greatly encouraged by the railway.

▲ Local freight survived on the northern section of the Grassington branch for nearly forty years after regular passenger services ended in 1930. Here, in 1966, a British Railways Standard Class 4MT locomotive, with a few open wagons in its care, waits to depart from Grassington's still intact station. Weeds and grass cover the track, a reminder that few trains came this way during the last years of this part of the line.

▼ In the summer of 1968, a year before closure, the Dalesman railtour train creeps along the overgrown track into Grassington station, with operations being directed by the smartly dressed station master. A few spectators, including the inevitable small boy, enjoy the rare sight of a passenger train at Grassington. With so many lines closing in the 1960s, special railtours such as this became a common event.

▼ From Swinden quarry southwards, the line is in fine shape, thanks to the continuing traffic from the limestone quarry. In 1979, when this picture was taken, the 1,100-tonne trains, with their special hopper wagons, were usually hauled by pairs of class 31 diesels, as shown here. Always a massive operation, the line has now carried over 4 million tonnes of stone.

► The line now ends at Swinden quarry, visible here in the distance, across the main road. After a short break, the old trackbed appears, now a home for geese and goats, happily grazing where the trains used to run. A bit farther on, a couple of stone bridges survive.

Freight was another matter, with the extensive traffic from a limestone quarry at Swinden, near Cracoe, a few miles south of Grassington. Closure of the section of the line from Swinden to Grassington came in August 1969, but from Skipton to Swinden the branch remains open, catering for much-expanded quarry traffic.

The lost and the living

From Swinden quarry to Grassington, cuttings, embankments and bridges make it simple to trace the route. With the great increase in road traffic, the Yorkshire Dales need more, not fewer, railways and there have been schemes to reopen the line to Grassington. At the other end of the branch, the Embsay & Bolton Abbey Railway has opened as a preserved line a section of the old Midland Railway route to Leeds. The atmosphere of this steam railway is similar to that of the Grassington branch in its heyday, while the Grassington branch today is home to massive stone trains hauled by modern diesels.

Abbey Town to Silloth

Through the 1850s a network of railways was built westwards from Carlisle along the southern shore of the Solway Firth. First, in 1854, came the line to Port Carlisle, along which – until 1914 – passengers were carried in a horse-drawn tram.

▲ A group of ladies in typical 1950s coats, and some other passengers hurry to board the train at Silloth station.

Next was an extension to Silloth, opened in 1856. A line went north across the firth to Annan on a spectacular two-mile viaduct. Supported on 193 piers, this was one of the great engineering achievements of the 1860s. Another link went southwards to Aspatria. This, in effect, turned the Silloth line into a short branch from Abbey Town.

Silloth at that time had busy docks and supported various local industries, including fishing. Despite all this, however, the line did not thrive, and in 1880 it was taken over by the North British Railway, resulting in the unusual situation of a railway situated in England being run by a Scottish company. Eventually, trade picked up as visitors were increasingly drawn to this remote region for its beaches, its wild landscape and its golf courses, and Silloth began to develop as a resort. A handsome small town built on a grid pattern, Silloth made the most of this new business. At the same time, the docks expanded, along with the local industries, notably flour milling. More freight traffic was attracted to the railway and so, by the end of the nineteenth century, the station and its extensive goods facilities covered a considerable

► Criffel Street, Silloth, as depicted on a 1904 postcard, at the height of the town's popularity as a resort, with plenty of elegant visitors and their carriages parading up and down. The distinctive architecture and the grid pattern of the streets can clearly be seen. To the left is the green, which spreads north towards the sea and the beaches. Little has changed today, except that the hotel is now called the Golf.

▼ Seeking out remains from Silloth's railway days is difficult, as little survives. Adjacent to the dock, however, is this old fence of weathered railway sleepers, looking not unlike a piece of environmental sculpture.

Cockermouth, Keswick and Penrith Railway.

TO

SILLOTH

INTRODUCTION OF
LIGHT-WEIGHT
DIESEL PASSENGER TRAINS

AMENDED
TRAIN SERVICE

CARLISLE
and
SILLOTH
and intermediate stations

29th NOVEMBER 1954
until further notice

(Subject to alteration)

◀ The Silloth branch was the first in Britain to have its steam trains replaced by the new diesel railcars, pioneers of a type of passenger vehicle that was soon to become universal on lesser and branch lines all over Britain. This British Railways leaflet advertises their introduction on 29 November 1954.

▲ Silloth's station and its extensive facilities, which included lines serving the docks and the flour mill, have almost all vanished, except for this building on the old platform. The main station building, to its left, was at one point converted into flats, but is now empty and abandoned.

C.16554   AERIAL VIEW, SILLOTH

▲ An aerial photograph of Silloth, taken in the 1950s, reveals the grid pattern of the streets, the large dock basin, the extensive network of railways around the station, and the large park-like green, with the beach beyond.

acreage. During World War II a big airfield outside Silloth also brought an increase in traffic.

In November 1954 the Silloth line saw new-style diesel multiple units being used for the first time on a British branch line. It was widely believed that the combination of their modern look and the rapid, clean and comfortable journeys that they offered would bring passengers back to the railways. However, by the end of that decade, traffic on the Silloth branch line was in decline, and in September 1964 the line was closed, along with the remaining parts of the Solway Firth network. Local opinion was determinedly against the closure, and there were protests and a even a sit-down on the line, but all to no avail.

Fading into history

Having been laid across a predominantly flat landscape, the railway has for the most part disappeared back into farmland. Little remains of Silloth station, although the docks survive in use and the flour mill is still busy. Traces of the trackbed can be seen from nearby minor roads, and some bridges survive, often isolated in the landscape. Most of the intermediate halts, usually adjacent to former level crossings, have become private houses. At Abbey Town, not far from the remains of the red stone abbey, the former junction has vanished almost entirely, absorbed back into the farmland.

◀ The old and the new, sitting side by side at Silloth station in the 1950s, when diesel railcars were a novelty. In the background is the flour mill, to the left the docks, the mainstays of the line through much of its history.

Derwent Valley Light Railway

The Light Railways Act of 1896 inspired many minor railways, the majority of which were rural or local branch lines aimed primarily at passenger traffic. Something rather different was the Derwent Valley Light Railway.

The 16-mile route from Layerthorpe, in York, to Cliffe Common, near Selby, was built between 1911 and 1913. Conceived largely as a freight line, it nevertheless had eleven stations, most of which were built in an appealing cricket-pavilion style. Its passenger services were operated by rudimentary railbuses. With connections at both ends and a meandering route that paralleled at a distance the direct line from York to Selby via Naburn, it had a certain

▲ On the outskirts of York, near Tang Hall, an old bridge over the former trackbed has been decorated with sculpture by Sustrans and with graffiti by local residents.

▼ The DVLR shed at York Layerthorpe, a ramshackle affair, was indicative of the somewhat primitive nature of much of the railway.

D. V. L. Rly.
RETURN HALF
Available for one Month only within one Month from date of issue
York L'thorpe
TO
WHELDRAKE
For conditions of issue see Company's Time Tables
SECOND CLASS
Fare 3/-

D. V. L. Rly.
OUTWARD HALF
Available on day of issue only.
WHELDRAKE
TO
YORK (L'THORPE)
For conditions of issue see Company's Time Tables
SECOND CLASS
Weldrake-York · Fare 3/-

◀ Murton Park station (formerly Wheldrake but rebuilt on its present site) is the headquarters of the Derwent Valley Light Railway preservation society. This shows the characteristic cricket pavilion-cum-bungalow style favoured by the DVLR in 1913 for its stations.

Menu.

SOUPS.

Oxtail.   Tomato.

FISH.

Boiled Cod   Shrimp Sauce.

JOINTS.

Roast Beef.   Horseradish Sauce.

Boiled Mutton.   Caper Sauce.

SWEETS.

Plum Pudding   Rum Sauce.

Cheese and Biscuits.

Celery.

Toast List.

"THE KING."

"THE DIRECTORS."
Proposer : Mr. S. J. Reading.
Responder : Mr. C. W. Thompson.

"SUCCESS TO THE D.V.L.R."
Proposer : Mr. L. Foster.
Responder : Major H. A. Watson, C.B.E.,
[M.V.O.

"DONORS AND VISITORS."
Proposer : Mr. H. J. Silke.
Responder : Mr. T. J. Vellacott.
[Messrs. Shell-Mex Ltd.].

"D.V. EMPLOYEES' SOCIAL CLUB."
Proposer : Mr. F. Cartledge.
Responder : Mr. W. J. Privett.

"HOST AND HOSTESS."
Proposer : Mr. J. A. Ratledge.

ENTERTAINMENT.
The following Artistes will entertain—
Messrs. Bob Machin, A. W. Gell,
P. Laycock.
Accompanied by Mr. A. Smith.

"God Save the King."

diversionary value, and was used in this way by the NER during World War I. Despite this, it had little appeal to the larger companies that surrounded it and so remained independent.

The DVLR managed to escape the Grouping of 1923 and, even more unusually, nationalization, and it never came under the control of British Railways. By then passenger services had long gone, having ceased on 1 September 1926, but there was enough freight (mostly agricultural – hence the DVLR was affectionately known as the Farmers' Line) to keep the railway open, and firmly in private hands, until the 1960s. In World War II it again proved its value as a diversionary route, but more important

▶ This is the menu and toast list used at a DVLR celebration dinner to mark the coronation of King George V in 1911. The diversity of toasts indicates the general spirit of optimism of that era.

▼ Freight trains continued to operate throughout the railway's life. Locomotives were ancient and the wagons were varied, adding to the character of this private railway. Here, a typical train passes Dunnington Halt.

▶ At a warehouse complex near Wheldrake, a short stretch of track survives in the tarmac, a reminder of the line's dependence upon goods traffic.

was its role in transporting bombs to the big RAF Bomber Command airfield at Elvington (now the Yorkshire Air Museum). It was said that the line's overgrown nature made it naturally camouflaged.

In 1964 British Railways closed the line from Selby to Hull, and the Derwent Valley's southern mainline link turned into a branch line. A year later the southern section, from Cliffe to Wheldrake, was closed, and then progressive closures took place up to 1973, by which time only the four miles from Dunnington to Layerthorpe remained open. Between 1977 and 1979 the railway's private owners operated regular steam services during the summer to attract tourists, and limited

DERWENT VALLEY LIGHT RAILWAY.
952 ONE DOG (Accompanied by Passenger) 952
At Co's Ltd. risk rate. See conditions on back.
YORK (Layerthorpe) to
For one journey under 10 miles. This ticket is available for a single journey only. Must be given up at destination station.
FARE 6d.

▼ Skipwith station has been delightfully restored. The two carriages adjoining it are used for holiday letting.

freight trains continued to run until 1981, at which point closure brought the story to an end. The remaining track was lifted soon after.

Today, despite its relatively recent demise, much of the route has gone. The northern section, from Layerthorpe to Osbaldwick, is part of a Sustrans cycle route. The next station, Murton Park, is the headquarters of the Derwent Valley Light Railway, a preservation society with a collection of locomotives and rolling stock, a fully restored DVLR station and a short length of track. South from here there is little to see, with the trackbed returned to the fields from which it came. Near Wheldrake are old warehouses and loading bays formerly linked to the railway. Skipwith station has been fully restored as a private house, complete with two carriages, while at the site of Cliffe Common there is an old platform and beyond it the grand junction station, also now a private dwelling.

▲ Cliffe Common was the southern end of the DVLR, where it met the Selby-to-Market Weighton line. All has gone save the big old station, which is now a private house, and a surviving section of overgrown platform.

▼ This distant view of Thorganby station, near the southern end of the line, was taken soon after it was opened. Passenger services were still operating (they finished in 1926) and the station buildings give a good sense of the economical nature of the line's structures.

Cockermouth to Sellafield

One of Britain's best railway journeys today is along the Cumbrian coast from Carlisle to Barrow, with its spectacular section from Maryport to Ravenglass virtually on the beach, overshadowed by hills and cliffs.

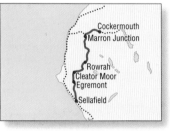

This line, the only one in this part of England, fights for survival physically and economically. Though isolated today, it was once the backbone of an extensive network spreading inland and linking remote places. Minerals were the inspiration, the lines making accessible huge deposits of iron ore and, later, haematite. The start, in the 1840s, was the Maryport & Carlisle Railway; others soon followed. The Whitehaven & Furness Junction built much of the coastal route, and the 1860s saw the completion of the route eastwards across the Lake District to Penrith, most of which was built by the Cockermouth, Keswick & Penrith Railway.

The development of this route, from Cockermouth south to the coast at Sellafield, was more fragmented. Things started in the south, with the opening in 1857 of the Whitehaven, Cleator & Egremont Railway. This had a slow start but as the mineral traffic developed it became very busy. Other local companies, such as the Cleator & Workington Junction, completed the network by the 1870s, with much of it eventually coming under the control of the ambitious Furness Railway. The ever-increasing importance of mineral traffic also inspired the building of some independent branches, such as the Rowrah & Kelton Fell Railway. However,

▲ It is a sunny day in about 1910 and all seems well with the world as Bridgefoot's stationmaster and a small boy pose for the camera. At this point passengers were still important on the route, but it was the mineral traffic that created the revenue.

▶ When lines disappear bridges carrying footpaths usually go as well, because they are no longer necessary. This elegant iron footbridge spanning the overgrown trackbed to the west of Cleator is, therefore, an unexpected survivor and a considerable rarity.

[146]

▲ Cockermouth's station has disappeared but, as this Edwardian photograph indicates, it was a substantial building reflecting various periods of expansion. As ever in photographs from this era, the people awaiting the train are all remarkably well dressed.

Between Ashby and Ullock the route of the railway can be seen as a low embankment running across the landscape against a magnificent backdrop of Lakeland hills.

the iron and haematite boom came to an end after World War I, so the lines began to close. The Rowrah branch had gone by 1927 and passenger traffic on the southern section ended in 1935. Closures were progressive from this point, and it all came to an end in 1966, when Cockermouth itself vanished from the network.

▼ Lines around Rowrah closed progressively from the late 1920s but some track was still in place in the 1960s. Here, the demolition gang is removing the last remains of what had been an extensive local network.

Despite these closures being relatively early, there is still plenty for the explorer to find. From Cockermouth south to Bridgefoot, roads have obliterated everything, but from here the route along the valley of the river Marron can be traced, with the section from Ullock to Wright Green being a footpath, offering wonderful views eastwards towards the Lake District. A low embankment that carried the line to Rowrah is still visible. Four lines met at Rowrah, and there is much still to be seen, though working it all out is rather

▼ Though no longer rail-connected (ridiculous though that seems), Egremont's massive Florence iron ore mine is still in operation. The old buildings give a hint of what the region must have been like when it was one of Britain's major iron ore and haematite producers.

complicated. The trackbed can then be traced to Cleator, with bridges and a station (now a private house) still in situ. The Sustrans Coast-2-Coast footpath crosses near Moor End. South of Cleator things are not so clear. A new bypass near Egremont has buried quite a bit but at Egremont the last link with the iron industry that for so long was the economic backbone of the region is to be found in Florence Mine, the deepest iron ore mine in Europe and still working, though no longer rail-connected. From here south to Thornhill the trackbed becomes a footpath and cycleway, and then it remains visible as an embankment south of Beckermet, where there was another iron ore branch. At Sellafield, in the shadow of the huge nuclear installation, the Cumbrian coast line brings back a railway reality.

[151]

Scotland

Castle Douglas to Kirkcudbright

South-west Scotland is now a region virtually without railways. There is a line northwards via Dumfries, and a meandering and slow route southwards from Glasgow to Stranraer, but everything in between was obliterated in the 1960s.

Kirkcudbright

◀ Kirkcudbright sits at the head of the tidal estuary of the Dee, a situation that explains both its importance as a fishing port and its appeal to visitors. This 1930s postcard shows this setting, and the compact nature of the town. The station was off the card to the left.

▼ Towards the end of the line's life, in the early 1960s, a two-coach local train crosses the Tongland viaduct over the River Dee on its way to Castle Douglas and Dumfries. It is hauled by a British Railways Standard tank locomotive of the kind used on minor railways all over Britain at this time. At this point the Dee is still tidal and the hydro-electric power station just upstream of the viaduct is used to maintain the water level.

Gone is the old direct route from Dumfries to Stranraer, via Castle Douglas and Newton Stewart, and with it its branches to Portpatrick, Whithorn and Kirkcudbright. Gone is any sense that Dumfries was the hub of a major railway network.

The Kirkcudbright Railway received authorization for its 10-mile line to Castle Douglas in 1861, and it opened three years later. In 1865 it was taken over by the Glasgow & South Western Railway, which continued to operate it until the Grouping of 1923. At this period there were through trains from London, taking between ten and twelve hours for the 371-mile journey from St Pancras. It then became part of LMS until the formation of British Railways in 1948. Throughout

▶ Kirkcudbright station was a handsome stone building, in keeping with the architecture of the town, and domestic in its appearance. Today nothing remains but the memory of all the people who passed through its doors over a century of railway use – including those exciting Glasgow colourist painters at the end of the nineteenth century.

◀ Today Tongland viaduct's piers and approach arches are still standing, their weathered stone suggesting something far older than the railway age. South of the bridge, a low embankment, which still exists among the trees, carried the line towards Kirkcudbright. To the north, little remains to be seen until Tongland is left behind.

this time extensive passenger and freight services kept the branch busy, particularly with fish traffic from Kirkcudbright's harbour. At the same time, there was a steady flow of tourists keen to explore the elegant streets of this handsome county town, whose busy and sharply tidal bay is overlooked by the ruins of sixteenth-century McLellan's Castle. It was from this harbour in 1622 that the first boatload of Scottish emigrants sailed for Nova Scotia. In the late 1800s painters from Glasgow regularly visited Kirkcudbright, drawn by the soft colours of the landscape, and Edward Hornel, one of the 'Glasgow Boys' group of artists, came to live here. The thriving artistic community that was established here still continues today. However, none of this was sufficient to keep the line open, and closure came in 1965, along with the rest of the network in this part of south-west Scotland.

▶ In addition to bridges and other railway structures that survive, more transient things can occasionally be spotted. This iron gatepost included a patent closing mechanism to ensure animals could not stray on to the track.

▼ On a rather gloomy August day in 1961, the local for Dumfries stands ready to depart from Kirkcudbright, headed by an LMS tank locomotive. The railway garden is flourishing and well cared for, the beds neatly edged with angled bricks, but the cast-iron name plate on the seat back already seems to have been removed by someone, although closure was still four years away.

Where to find the evidence

Since closure, much of the line has returned into the gentle green landscape whence it came. Despite this, plenty does survive and the route can be followed and readily identified from adjacent roads. A short stretch a little south of Castle Douglas is an official footpath, allowing for close inspection of bridges and other structures, which often feature attractive detailing in local stone. Some stations exist, now converted to private houses or offices, for example Bridge of Dee and Tarff. Some sections have been buried by road improvement schemes, but elsewhere, notably north of Tongland, the route can clearly be traced on the wooded hillside on the east side of the road. The main engineering feature was the viaduct that carried the line across the Dee to the south of Tongland.

▲ Near Mollance the embankment that carried the railway is clearly visible, with the remains of a small bridge. Beyond the bridge the embankment has vanished, giving the concrete remains, now the province of sheep, a curious kind of abstraction. In the distance are the hills that provide a magnificent backdrop for much of the route.

The approach arches and piers that carried this still stand, just to the north of the old arched road bridge. From here into Kirkcudbright the line becomes harder to distinguish, with much having been obliterated by housing and road schemes. Originally it came to an end in a big station yard overlooking the Dee's tidal estuary, to the north of the harbour and the town centre. Here, it is hard to find any evidence to indicate that Kirkcudbright once had a railway, let alone one that existed for just over a century.

Roxburgh to Jedburgh

High in the list of regions of Britain most devastated by the railway closures of the 1960s is the Scottish Borders. A large area south of Edinburgh is now devoid of any rail service whatsoever.

Jedburgh Abbey

Included in the slaughter was the old North British line from Coldstream to St Boswells via Roxburgh, an area famous for its castles and abbeys. From Roxburgh a 7-mile branch ran south to Jedburgh, along the banks of the Teviot and Jed Water. Built independently and opened in July 1856, it was taken

▼ Freight services survived on the Jedburgh branch until the 1960s and were very regular in the late 1950s, when this photograph was taken of Jedburgh station yard. The locomotive waits while a porter loads goods into a wagon. One of Jedburgh's major industries was textiles, and the factories were busy users of the line. Today, nothing of this remains.

◄ This romantic view of Jedburgh Abbey, set above the river, was issued as a postcard in the 1920s, one of a series called 'Ruined Abbeys'.

► Jedburgh station is buried beneath a modern industrial estate. It was never a grand station and, by the time this photograph was taken in the late 1950s, it had a tired air, a consequence of the ending of passenger services several years earlier.

◄ All that remains of Jedfoot station are two platforms. One, flanking the trackbed that at this point is part of the Border Abbeys Way, is in good order, with stone edging. The other is decrepit and overgrown, but visibly formed from old sleepers set vertically. Nearby is a pile of telegraph poles, abandoned when the line closed, and in the bushes are the remains of the level-crossing gates.

over by the North British Railway in 1860. Through the rest of the nineteenth century and into the twentieth, the line was the main gateway to this county town and royal borough, famous for its abbey and its castle, and its associations with Mary, Queen of Scots, who stayed here in 1566. Other famous visitors included William Wordsworth and Sir Walter Scott; the latter made his first appearance as an advocate in a criminal trial here in 1793. Another of the town's claims to fame is the invention of seven-a-side rugby.

The railway survived into the time of British Railways, but in August 1948 disaster struck as floods seriously damaged the track. Passenger services ceased at once, but basic repairs enabled freight trains to run until 1964. Today, in Jedburgh itself there is little sign of the railway. The site of the station and the goods yard has vanished beneath an industrial park, but the trackbed is apparent as it leaves the town past the rugby club's field. From this point, it is easily discernible in the landscape and, considering the early date of closure to passengers, there is plenty to be seen, including station houses and platforms at Nisbet and Kirkbank, both now private, and a platform at Jedfoot. Here, and elsewhere, the trackbed is a part of the Borders Abbeys Way. Never far from the river, the route is an enjoyable walk, especially on the approach to Roxburgh with the grand arches of the Teviot viaduct in the distance.

Killin Junction to Loch Tay

The appeal of the history and the landscape of Scotland, and Scottish rivers and lochs in particular, increased steadily through the latter years of the Victorian era, encouraged both by literature and by increasing accessibility.

THE FALLS OF DOCHART. KILLIN

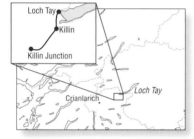

It was the expanding railway network that really opened the country up to visitors. Typical was the region around the river Tay, with Loch Tay itself being served by two separate railways. One was the 5-mile Killin Railway, opened in 1886 to link the western end of Loch Tay with the Caledonian Railway's main line westwards from

▲ The Falls of Dochart, on the river Dochart just to the south of Killin and only a short walk from the town, is a famous feature of the region, and has been a popular draw for tourists since the Victorian era. The railway ran just behind the cottages on the left, and so the falls would have been visible, and audible, from the train.

Dunblane to Oban via Crianlarich. Operated by the Caledonian and later by the LMS, this was primarily a tourist line, with its terminus on the shores of Loch Tay by the steamer pier. When the steamer service was withdrawn in September 1939, passenger carrying beyond Killin also ended. The rest of the line lived on into British Railways' time and survived until September 1965.

Today there is much to be seen. The trackbed is visible, and walkable, to the site of the Loch Tay terminus. Killin station has gone, along with most of the route through the town. However, beyond the spectacular Falls of Dochart, one of the area's main attractions, the trackbed becomes a well-defined footpath that climbs gently through the surrounding forests to Killin Junction. Here, isolated in the silence of the forest, the two lines, both now footpaths, converge by the surviving platform. Beyond are the remains of derelict railway cottages, the only clue to the busy past of this delightful and secret place.

▼ (*Inset*) The Killin branch follows the river Dochart on its way to Loch Tay. Beyond Killin Junction, the line westwards to Crianlarich continues along Glen Dochart. This 1920s view gives a sense of the magnificent setting enjoyed by the railway.

▼ The Killin branch was built partly to encourage tourism, and the original route served a steamer pier at the western end of Loch Tay, which was also the terminus of the branch, with a small station and a engine shed. Passenger services ceased on this section in 1939, but the trackbed can still be seen in places, raised above the Loch's shore and beyond the boulders in this photograph.

GLEN DOCHART, KILLIN

◀ As the branch approaches the end of its life in the 1960s, a single-coach train drops down towards Killin from the junction, hauled by a former Caledonian tank locomotive, now in British Railways livery. This type of engine was in use on the branch for much of its life. The classic branch line scene could be anywhere in Britain but, ironically, since the closure of the Killin line, extensive conifer forestation has given the route a much more typically Scottish look.

Dunblane to Crianlarich

Railways came comparatively early to Perth, with a number of lines either authorized or in operation during the 1840s. Typical was the Dundee & Perth, opened in May 1847.

As a result, Perth became a busy railway centre and the meeting point for trains operated by the Highland, Caledonian and North British companies. The most important route was the line running northwards to Inverness, and south to Glasgow and Edinburgh via Dunblane and Stirling. A number of other lines connected with this, including the Dunblane, Doune & Callander Railway. This small independent company was launched

◀ This Edwardian card of Lochearnhead richly evokes the colours of the Highlands. In the distance, steam rises from a train crossing Ogle Burn viaduct, on the line from Perth to Oban via Crieff. The next station on the line, Lochearnhead, survives, almost complete.

◀ Until its closure in the 1960s, the Dunblane to Crianlarich section of the old Callander & Oban line was a busy route, taking substantial trains. Here, on a sunny day in the early 1960s a 5MT locomotive leaves Callander at the head of the Oban to Glasgow service.

▲ Much of Balquhidder station remains, including classical-style stonework, decorative ironwork and a generously proportioned, white-tiled passage connecting the platforms. Structures of this quality were typical of the line; those that remain are fitting memorials.

in 1846 but it took some years to build its short line and did not open until 1858. It was to enjoy its independence for only a few years and by 1865 had been absorbed into the Caledonian's network. For some time Callander was to remain the end of the line, but by 1865 the Caledonian had decided to extend westwards, towards Oban, by giving support to another nominally independent company, the Callander & Oban Railway. Always short of money, this company built its line in short bursts, waiting in the meantime for more Caledonian support. The first impromptu terminus was at Killin and the next at Dalmally, but Oban was finally reached and the line opened throughout in 1880. Callander therefore boasted two stations, subsequently known as Callander East (the original one) and Callander

Dreadnought. A few years later the West Highland line from the Clyde to Fort William was completed, meeting the Callander & Oban at Crianlarich. In fact, operated as they were by rival companies, they did not quite meet, but crossed, necessitating two stations at Crianlarich (Upper and Lower). Other lines were built, including an alternative route to Perth via Crieff, which left the Callander & Oban at Balquhidder, and a short branch to Killin and Loch Tay. Everything remained in place until the 1960s, when all the lines eastwards from Crianlarich were closed.

The route today

Built through a remote and underpopulated region, much of the railway's route from Dunblane to Crianlarich can still be traced. Plenty survives, both on the map and in the landscape, so exploration is easy. A long section, from Callander to Balquhidder, is part of the National Cycle Network, and there are plans to extend this. And part of the route west from Balquhidder, including the Killin branch, is a footpath. This winds through hills and forest, close to the River Leny through the Pass of Leny, with distant mountain and moorland views. Linking paths offer detours to Loch Earn and Loch Tay. Along the line, there are the remains of stations and other buildings to be seen, with notable examples at Balquhidder and Killin Junction. At the latter, a long curving, grass-covered platform stands alone in a delightful setting, surrounded by woodland. Only the ruins of old stone-built cottages and an overgrown iron gate or two give any hint that this was, until 1965, a busy railway junction, noisy with the sound of trains and visitors on outings to Loch Tay.

◀ Killin Junction is now the meeting point for two footpaths. On the left in the distance is the trackbed of the old Killin branch, while on the right the former line towards Dunblane climbs away into the trees. In the foreground the platform remains, but all other traces of the railway junction and its station have gone.

► In 1961 two diesels haul a four-coach train through the rugged landscape of Glen Ogle. The route demanded powerful locomotives to cope with the terrain and the winter snow.

▼ While much of the route through Glen Ogle is cut into the rocky hillside, at one point the line is carried on two hefty stone viaducts. Built in 1870 and matching the wild and powerful nature of the landscape, these are unusual in running parallel to the slope. They now carry a footpath and cycleway.

Aberdeen to Ballater

Famous for its associations with Queen Victoria and Balmoral, the 43-mile-long Deeside branch to Ballater had a chequered history.

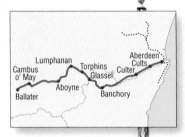

The Deeside Railway was authorized to build a line from Aberdeen to Aboyne in 1846. By 1853 this was open only half way, to Banchory. Another company was then formed, the Deeside Extension Railway, to complete the line to Aboyne, which it did in 1859. Six years later yet another company, the Aboyne & Braemar, took over the baton, so to speak, and in October 1866 the railway reached Ballater. It never continued to Braemar, partly because the planned route went close to Balmoral and would have affected the

▼ Cults, a few miles west of Aberdeen, was one of a large number of small stations along the line, many of which had goods facilities, as this picture shows. Some of the smallest were restricted in use and untimetabled. It is easy to imagine the royal train dashing through the station.

▶ Near Crathes a stretch of track has been laid, adjacent to a restaurant and conference centre. Some carriages and a diesel shunter reside here. The track soon peters out in the woods to the west, but the trackbed continues towards Banchory. At one time Crathes Castle had a private halt.

▼ Jubilee class no. 45730, 'Ocean', waits to take its train out of Aberdeen's city centre station, the start of the journey to Ballater. The branch line swung west at Ferryhill Junction, to the north of the city, and then continued for miles along the Dee valley into an ever more remote and empty landscape.

royal family's privacy. Another scheme, to build a line from Ballater to Inverness, also came to nought. In the 1870s everything came under the control of the Great North of Scotland Railway. Frequent use by the royal family gave the line a certain standing and special trains ran regularly until the 1930s, carrying dispatches to Aberdeen to catch the London train. In 1904 the GNSR instituted a bus service from Ballater to Braemar.

Although the route westwards from Aberdeen passed through increasingly wild and underpopulated scenery, there were plenty of stations, 26 in all, including some with restricted use, such as the delightfully named Aboyne Curling Pond Platform. In due course the line passed to the LNER and thence to British Railways, who tried out battery-powered railcars in the late 1950s with some success. The royal connection helped to keep the branch open, but in the end economics prevailed and it closed in 1966.

Forty years on there is still plenty to see. Between Cults and Banchory the line followed the Dee and the overgrown trackbed is visible from the accompanying road. Near Crathes, where there is a restaurant and conference centre, some track has been relaid and carriages and a diesel shunter are in residence. Banchory station has gone but from here to Aboyne the landscape is more open and embankments, cuttings and bridges are all to be seen. From Aboyne the route is by the A93. Dinnet station is remarkably complete and is used as an estate office, while at Ballater the restored station houses shops, the local tourist office and a café.

▲ West of Banchory the landscape opens out and the trackbed is, for the most part, clear. Here, even the old railway fencing survives, flanking the track towards the line of distant hills.

◀ Banchory, which for a while in the 1850s was the end of the line, was a grand and complex station, as this old photograph indicates. Nothing remains today.

▶ Ballater station was never planned as a terminus as the line was meant to continue westwards, so it is a simple wooden building, now housing shops, a café and a tourist office.

Exploring Lost Lines

RAILWAY RAMBLERS (www.railwayramblers.org.uk)

Many have discovered the pleasures of walking old railway lines, an activity that combines an enjoyment of landscape with a sense of history and the chance of finding interesting railway structures and relics. Railway Ramblers was founded in 1978 by a group of amateur railway explorers fired by the ambition to discover and document all abandoned railways. At that time there were only about 250 miles of official railway paths in Britain and thousands of miles of closed lines, many by then in private hands. Planning walks for members was, therefore, a complex operation involving gaining permissions from many landowners, often with differing attitudes towards railway exploration. Since then the club has grown steadily; regional branches have been established, and they plan their own programmes of walks. David Shepherd OBE became president and Bill Pertwee vice-president, and the quarterly newsletter is now substantial, with numerous reports of

◀ Railway Ramblers take lunch on a bridge near Stichen, during a walk in 2002 along the line from Maud Junction towards Fraserburgh, Aberdeenshire.

▲ Few closed railways still have track in place but in 1991 it could be enjoyed at Lavant, on the old line from Chichester to Midhurst, in West Sussex.

recent explorations. The result is that all abandoned lines have been discovered and many are documented, but plenty remains to be done. Railway Ramblers has also been a significant fundraiser in this field and contributions have been made to Sustrans and other organizations to help purchase rail routes and convert them into footpaths and cycleways. Donations have also helped to preserve viaducts and other structures. Now well past its quarter century, Railway Ramblers is still pursuing its original aims, and it continues to offer to like-minded enthusiasts the chance to explore and enjoy Britain's railway past.

▼ Prysor viaduct, one of the glories of the old GWR line from Blaenau Ffestiniog to Bala, in Wales, is visited by a group from the Yorkshire branch of Railway Ramblers.

◀ Distinctive and individual mileposts mark each Sustrans route. This example is near Cleator Moor, on a former railway in Cumbria.

▼ One of the most popular routes is the Camel Trail in Cornwall, an ideal journey along the former railway from Bodmin to Padstow.

SUSTRANS (www.sustrans.org.uk)

Sustrans, known originally as Sustainable Transport, was founded in Bristol in 1977 with a determination to face the problems caused by the uncontrolled growth of road traffic. The organization's primary aim was to campaign for the creation of a national network of cyclepaths all over Britain, to make it easier for people to use sustainable transport. Many paths were to be based on abandoned railway lines, and the Bristol & Bath Railway Path was the start. Since then, the National Cycle Network has grown steadily and the original target of 10,000 miles has been achieved. Today it is a huge, nationwide network of signed cycling and walking routes linking schools, stations, city centres and diverse areas of the British countryside. About one-third of the network is traffic-free. Sustrans coordinates the work of the many organizations that are creating new routes, both local and long-distance. By raising funds on a national scale, it is able to buy or lease the necessary land, construct routes to a high standard, replace missing bridges and structures, identify the routes with seats and markers (often commissioned from artists and crafts people), and establish long-term maintenance schemes. Sustrans has incorporated hundreds of miles of former railways into its routes, greatly increasing awareness of, and access to, Britain's greatest legacy from the railway age.

Picture Credits

The Author

Paul Atterbury is a lifelong railway enthusiast who has always appreciated the power of railway ephemera – such as postcards, timetables and tickets – to tell the story of Britain's railway past. Familiar to many as a long-standing member of the team of experts on BBC TV's *Antiques Roadshow*, Paul's previous railway books include *Discovering Britain's Lost Railways, Branch Line Britain, Along Country Lines, Tickets Please!, Along Lost Lines, All Change, Life Along the Line, Along Main Lines* and *An A–Z of Railways.*

Index

Index

Index